MW00563265

Forecasting for the Pharmaceutical Industry

Forecasting for the Pharmaceutical Industry

Models for New Product and In-Market Forecasting and How to Use Them

ARTHUR G. COOK, PH.D.

ZS ASSOCIATES

GOWER

Published by
Gower Publishing Limited
Gower House
Croft Road
Aldershot
Hampshire
GU11 3HR
England

Gower Publishing Company
Suite 420
101 Cherry Street
Burlington
VT 05401-4405
USA

Arthur G. Cook has asserted his moral right under the Copyright, Designs and Patents Act, 1988, to be identified as the author of this work.

British Library Cataloguing in Publication Data
Cook, Arthur G.
   Forecasting for the pharmaceutical industry
   1.Pharmaceutical industry – Forecasting 2.Drugs – Marketing
   3.Drugs – Research – Forecasting
   I.Title
   338.4'761519'0112

   ISBN-10: 0 566 08675 1
   ISBN-13: 978-0-566-08675-5

Library of Congress Cataloging-in-Publication Data
Cook, Arthur G.
   Forecasting for the pharmaceutical industry : models for new product
and in-market forecasting and how to use them / by Arthur G. Cook.
      p. cm.
   Includes bibliographical references and index
   ISBN 0-566-08675-1 (alk. paper)
   1. Pharmaceutical industry--Forecasting. 2. Pharmaceutical industry.
I.Title
   [DNLM: 1. Drug Industry--trends. 2. Forecasting--methods.
QV 736 C771f 2006]
HD9665.5.C666 2006
615.1068'4--dc22

2006012223

Printed and bound in Great Britain by TJ International Ltd, Padstow, Cornwall.

Contents

List of Figures

List of Tables

List of Abbreviations

CNS   –   central nervous system

COGS   –   cost of goods sold

DOTs   –   days of therapy

EU   –   European Union

HIV   –   Human Immunodeficiency Virus

NPV   –   net present value

NRx   –   new prescriptions

R&D   –   research and development

Rx   –   prescription

TRx   –   total prescriptions

US   –   United States of America

Acknowledgements

One of the central tenets of forecasting is that collaboration leads to better insights and results. The same is true of writing, and I gratefully acknowledge the many co-workers over the years who have helped to shape this text. I also wish to acknowledge Michael German whose artistic prose added much of the 'human element' to the PharmaCo Case Study

My colleagues over the years, from University days to Syntex Pharmaceuticals to ZS Associates have provided me – constantly and consistently – with both the intellectual challenge and reality checks that have led to many of the approaches discussed in this text. Balance is a key to success in many ventures, and I have been fortunate to be exposed to people who exemplify dynamic balance. Industry experience at Syntex Pharmaceuticals brought me from the real business into the academic best practices domain. Consulting experience at ZS Associates has translated intellectual rigour into practical application. Without my colleagues educating me in both these approaches this book would not have been possible.

In particular I am grateful to BN, AW and RB for their friendship, intellectual challenge and practicality checks over the years. Without their constant support, encouragement, friendship and honesty this text never would have been written.

Foreword

What is a forecast? Potential answers to this question is as diverse as the many different functional roles within a company and include:

- Forecasting is an accurate picture of the future.
- Forecasting represents the best judgement of the future.
- Forecasting serves as a framework for interpreting present events.
- Forecasting identifies factors with which the corporation must cope.
- Forecasting provides a sorting rule among corporate choices.
- Forecasting forces examination of current strategic assumptions.
- Forecasting sets up guideposts to mark the path into the future.
- Forecasting offers aid in decision-making.
- Forecasting offers directions for action.
- Forecasting is a measure of uncertainty.
- Forecasting combines art and science.
- Forecasting is not an exercise in mathematics; it is an expression of the art of management.

With which of these views do you agree? The answer will depend on your perspective. If you are looking at resource trade-offs in an R&D pipeline, you may view forecasting as the keystone of strategic portfolio planning. If you are developing tactical marketing plans, the forecast may be a tool to gauge the financial results of specific tactics. If you are in charge of manufacturing, you may look to the forecast to provide accurate direction for the number of units that must be manufactured. This simple question – 'What is a forecast?' – illustrates the key challenge of forecasting: the need to provide inputs for multiple decisions within an organisation.

This book addresses the varied elements of forecasting. It is organised into six chapters. In Chapter 1, we examine the history of forecasting and the lessons that can be applied to the practice of forecasting in the pharmaceutical industry. In Chapter 2, we examine the tools, methods and analytics that are available to the forecaster. In Chapters 3 and 4, we discuss the detailed approaches and algorithms that can be used in new product and in-market forecasting. In Chapter 5 we conclude the main text with our forecast of forecasting – that is, thoughts on the future of forecasting. Chapter 6 provides a case study to help the reader apply the forecasting concepts.

1

The Past and the Present

CHAPTER 1

The Past and the Present

Things are more like they are now than they ever were before.

Dwight D. Eisenhower

The future is like the present – only longer.

Goose Gossage

THE INACCURACY OF FORECASTING

Predicting the future is difficult. A historical look at forecasting over time suggests that we have continually tried to predict the future ... and have continually failed to do so with any accuracy:

The telephone has too many shortcomings to be seriously considered as a means of communication. The device is inherently of no value to us.
Western Union internal memo, 1876

People will tire of talkers. Talking is no substitute for the good acting we had in silent pictures.
Thomas Alva Edison, 1925, on new movies with sound

Predicting the future is difficult.

Every woman is frightened of a mouse.
MGM head Louis B. Mayer in 1926, to a young cartoonist named Walt Disney

I think there is a world market for maybe five computers.
Thomas Watson, IBM Chairman, 1943

The band's OK but, if I were you, I'd get rid of the singer with the tyre-tread lips.
BBC radio producer on rejecting the Rolling Stones at a 1963 audition

How could the experts get it so wrong?

The concept is interesting and well-formed, but in order to earn better than a 'C', the idea must be feasible.
A business professor at Yale on the FedEx marketing plan, 1966

640k ought to be enough for anybody.
Bill Gates, Microsoft founder, 1981

The Internet will collapse within a year.
Bob Metcalf, founder of 3Com Corporation, in December 1995

We look at these examples today and chuckle – how could the experts get it so wrong? But we have the advantage of hindsight. At the time the comments were made, they surely reflected the current thinking of these individuals and organisations. The simple lesson – that even the experts get it wrong – is a good one to bear in mind as we review in later chapters the role of expert judgement in forecasting.

A more subtle – and just as important – lesson is to reflect upon the pressures that must have existed on the forecaster in industries associated with the individuals who made these statements. If I am a forecaster for Internet equipment and the chairman of 3Com has made a public statement that he believes the Internet will collapse within a year, chances are that I will be affected by this statement in my view of the future. We will discuss the issue of bias in forecasting in each of the subsequent chapters.

Are companies any better at forecasting than individual experts? The results in Table 1.1 suggest that companies also have a mixed record when it comes to forecasting. Table 1.1 presents some new products that have been introduced by large companies and categorises the products as 'leaders' and 'laggards' with respect to their relative success in the global markets. These companies all have successful new product launches to their credit, but they also introduced products to the market with limited success. It is reasonable to assume that the planning for the new products included forecasts that presumably justified the product launches. What went wrong? We will explore the answer to this question when we discuss new product forecasting in Chapter 3.

Table 1.1 The success of new product introductions

Company	Leaders	Laggards
McDonald's	Big Mac and fries	Seaweed burgers
Sony	Walkman	Beta-format VCRs
Kodak	35mm photography	Instant photography
Federal Express	Overnight mail	ZapMail
Coke	Classic Coke	New Coke

FORECASTING IN THE PHARMACEUTICAL INDUSTRY

What about examples from the pharmaceutical industry? In 1985 there was an article published in *Pharmaceutical Executive* that examined the linkage between successful new product launches and a company's stock price. The authors stated that

> *Projections of the sales of new drugs, especially of blockbuster drugs, have almost always been too high. Investors have been burned so many times with this game that it is difficult to understand why they continue to play it.*[1]

In support of this statement have a look at the data in Table 1.2.

Table 1.2 Blockbusters that went bust

Company	Drug name	Peak sales (millions of US dollars)	
		Estimated	Actual
Merck	Blocarden	500–1000	15
A. H. Robbins	Pondamin	300	3
Sterling	Amrinone (oral)	500	0
SmithKline	Monocid	100	20

At the other end of the scale are products that achieved forecasts beyond their initial expectations (see Table 1.3). These examples are offered as evidence that some blockbuster drugs are not recognised as such when initially forecast.

Projections of the sales of new drugs, especially of blockbuster drugs, have almost always been too high.

1   Riccardo, J. P. and Ryan, B. (1985) 'Minimizing the Risks', *Pharmaceutical Executive*, November, 74–6.

THE PAST AND
THE PRESENT

Table 1.3   Beyond expectations

| | | Peak sales (millions of US dollars) | |
Company	Drug name	Estimated	Actual
Upjohn	Motrin	25	200
Schering-Plough	Garamycin	6–8	300
Syntex	Naprosyn	40–50	420
SmithKline	Tagamet	200	1000
Upjohn	Xanax	30–40	200
Marion	Cardizem	50	180
Searle	Aspartame	0	585

The accuracy of a forecast is highly dependent upon the the datapoints used in the comparison of 'actual' to 'forecast' performance.

The data in Tables 1.2 and 1.3 are those cited in the 1985 article in *Pharmaceutical Executive*. Had they been updated for sales after 1985 the discrepancy between forecast and actual performance would be even greater.

Do we have more recent examples than those from 1985? Unfortunately, no. The pharmaceutical industry has become more circumspect about publishing internal company estimates of forecast potential for new products. The speed with which financial – and increasingly legal – markets respond to forecasts has dissuaded pharmaceutical companies from publishing internal forecast data. Moreover, the accuracy of a forecast is highly dependent upon the datapoints used in the comparison of 'actual' to 'forecast' performance. For example, actual performance of a product – compared to its forecast one month previously – is typically more accurate than actual performance compared to a forecast from two years previously. Without knowing the time period of the comparison, claims of forecast accuracy cannot be judged.

Although we have no concrete public data by which to judge the accuracy of forecasting in the pharmaceutical industry, we do have some indicators. In January 2004 an article in *MedAdNews* presented a list of 'future blockbusters', as shown in Table 1.4.[2] As time progresses, comparing actual data for these products relative to their forecast data will give us an indication of what improvements – if any – have occurred in forecasting pharmaceutical products between 1985 and the present. Of course, the best source of data lies within each company, and readers of this text from within the pharmaceutical industry will be able to judge their company's relative success in pharmaceutical forecasting from review of these internal data.

---

2   Humphreys, A. (2004) 'Future Blockbusters', *MedAdNews*, January, 1–12.

Table 1.4   Future pharmaceutical blockbusters?

Product	Manufacturer	Use	Projected peak sales (millions of US dollars)
Avastin	Genentech	Cancer	3000
Exanta	AstraZeneca	Thrombosis	1300
Alvesco	Altana, Aventis	Asthma	1200
Arcoxia	Merck	Osteoarthritis	2500
Caduet	Pfizer	Hypertension, hypercholesterolemia	1090
Cymbalta	Lilly	Depression	2200
Zocor/Zetia	Merck, Schering-Plough	Cholesterol	3000
Genasense	Genta	Malignant melanoma	900
Lyrica	Pfizer	Neuropathic pain	2000
Spiriva	Boehringer Ingelheim, Pfizer	Pulmonary disease	1340

History, clearly, provides few comprehensive and simple solutions for forecasting in the future. The lessons of history, however, do provide us with the insights that have led to the best practices we will discuss in the remainder of this book. Before moving on to these solutions, let's examine the current state of forecasting with respect to its role in pharmaceutical companies. This current state also drives many of the best practices we will discuss.

THE CURRENT STATE: INFLUENCES ACROSS FUNCTIONS

Forecasting feeds into and influences many other functional areas within an organisation (see Figure 1.1). These linkages may be unidirectional (where forecasts feed into decisions made by the other functional areas) or bidirectional (where the forecast is used to quantify the effects of market changes envisioned by other functional areas). The links reflect the varied uses to which a forecast can be applied – such as revenue planning, production planning, resource allocation, project prioritisation, partnering decisions, compensation plans, lobbying efforts and so forth. These varied uses, and the effect of forecasting on many functional areas in an organisation, reflect the

Forecasting feeds into and influences many other functional areas within an organisation (see Figure 1.1)..

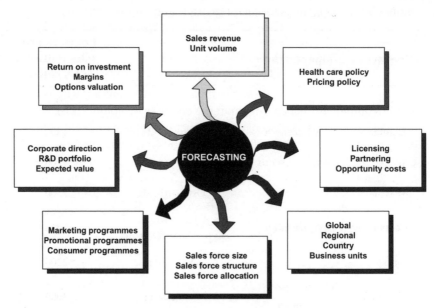

Figure 1.1   Forecast links to other functional areas

first major challenge of forecasting – meeting the needs of varied and diverse stakeholders.

The link between forecasting sales revenue and unit volume is an obvious one; however, the form of the forecast required may differ between these two. The unit volume forecast needs to include detail above that required for revenue demand – including information on sampling units, safety stock and the distribution of product amongst the various packaging forms. These links should be bidirectional. In other words, the forecaster must understand the needs of the recipients of the forecast in order to select the best methods for generating the forecast (there is more on this in Chapters 3 and 4).

Links to health care and pricing policy typically take the form of 'what if' scenarios. Questions such as 'What is the effect on product demand if a (specific) health care policy is enacted?' or 'What is the effect on demand if we launch at a 10 per cent higher cost per day of therapy than originally planned?' fall into this category. In essence a change in the market environment (health care policy) or a change in price needs to be quantified by the forecaster. This example is also bidirectional; the appropriate functional area provides the input scenarios and assumptions to the forecaster, who then quantifies the results and provides direction back to the other functional areas.

In most organisations the role of business development (identifying and evaluating licensing, co-marketing, and co-promotion opportunities) relies upon the ability to quantify these opportunities – a forecasting function. As with the previous examples, the information flow needs to be bidirectional between the functional areas and as before the form of a business development forecast varies for each function. In business development forecasts there is more of a focus on what each partner contributes to overall product success, and what incremental gains might be made through co-promotion opportunities.

From these three examples it already is apparent that a 'forecast' will have different requirements depending upon the end user – a volume forecast at the package level, a 'what if' scenario construct to evaluate different policy options, or a forecast that explicitly evaluates the contributions of two companies to a product's revenue potential. These differing requirements add to the complexity of what is required of a forecast. Let's continue to add to this complexity by examining the other functional area requirements.

Forecasting complexity

Forecasts may be done at a global, regional, country, or business unit level. Each forecast has differing levels of data required, both at the input and output level. These forecasts need different structural constructs – for example, if doing a regional forecast for a product in Europe do I assume one European launch date or individual launch dates in each of the key countries? Is there a 'pan-European' adoption curve for the product or should individual country's adoption patterns be modelled? The answer to these, and many other, questions dictate the design of the forecast model.

In the sales and marketing areas, forecasts are used to drive resource allocation decisions. What products are the most responsive to sales and marketing efforts? What is the effect on the product forecast when sales or marketing resources are changed? These promotion–response requirements lead to a different construction of the forecast than that required for the other functional areas. These flows are bidirectional – changes in the initially assumed resource level are analysed and the forecast adjusted appropriately.

From these three examples it already is apparent that a 'forecast' will have different requirements depending upon the end user

Forecasts used for research and development (R&D) portfolio planning also require different constructs and outputs than the other functional areas. In these types of forecasts we need to adjust for risk and uncertainty in the forecast (there is more about this in Chapter 2). Modelling the responsiveness of product potential to changes in the R&D resource allocation requires similar questions to the process of modelling the best use of sales and marketing resources, but the process of analysis is slightly different. As previously, the needs of the functional area drive the forecast construct.

Finally, forecasts feed into the finance function: various financial ratios – such as net present value, return on investment, breakeven dates, and so forth – need to be calculated from the forecast revenues. Although this flow, in theory, is unidirectional the financial requirements of an organisation (for example, earnings per share) sometimes feed back into the forecast to drive a change in revenue projection. The application of options valuation techniques – long used in assessing the equities markets – are starting to find a place in pharmaceutical product forecasting. These techniques also create requirements for the forecast construct.

Thus, the many functional areas that interact with the forecast create tremendous pressure on the model construct, the analytics, the inputs and the outputs of the forecast. In other words, every function develops its own model, based on a different set of assumptions with little or no consistency across the board. The key challenge to forecasting is to create a process where the needs of function can be met without compromising the integrity of the forecast approach.

THE TIME HORIZON FOR THE FORECAST

A second key challenge in forecasting arises from the varied time horizons associated with a forecast. Forecasts range from very long-term time horizons (for example, a ten-year forecast for a product that will launch three years from now) to a short-term focus (quarterly forecasts that will be used to set incentive compensation goals for the sales organisation). There are a variety of time points between these two examples, as shown in Figure 1.2.

The time horizon for the forecast has implications for the choice of forecasting method and model construction. Splitting an annual forecast for a product into a monthly forecast is a complex task. Ensuring that the 'exit' forecast for one year and the 'entrance' forecast for the subsequent year result in a smooth transition is difficult. Creating this transition, while maintaining a reasonable growth trajectory throughout a year, is a challenge to the forecaster.

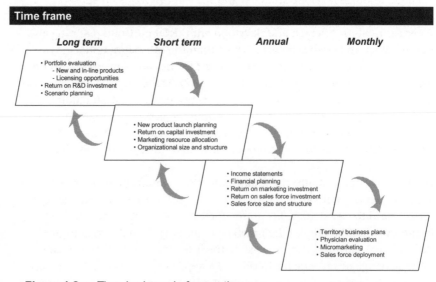

Figure 1.2 Time horizons in forecasting

Similarly, creating a multi-year long-term forecast at the monthly level can be a challenge. The rolling up of monthly outputs to annual totals is not difficult, but the number of data inputs and outputs can be cumbersome to manage. A ten-year forecast at the monthly level would have 120 datapoints for each input and output variable.

IN SUMMARY

This chapter discussed some of the challenges to forecasting and some of the lessons we have learned from a retrospective look at forecasting across several industries: the many and varied stakeholders in forecasting lead to a number of different pressures on the forecast and the forecaster. The need for forecasts that span multiple years as well as forecasts that are used for monthly planning creates another balance point which the forecaster must consider. The remainder of this book will address these challenges head on – presenting tools and methods that can be employed in delivering the appropriate forecast.

This chapter discussed some of the challenges to forecasting and some of the lessons we have learned from a retrospective look at forecasting.

The Forecasting Process

*In this chapter
we will examine
best practices
in forecasting,
the methods
available to
the forecaster
and analytic
tools that can
be used across
forecasting
methodologies.*

*Far better an approximate answer to the right question, which is often vague,
than an exact answer to the wrong question, which can be made precise.*

Tukey

Tell the truth and you will get your head bashed in.

Hungarian proverb

In Chapter 1 we discussed the need for forecasts in the pharmaceutical
industry and the role of forecasts in driving decision-making across a
variety of different functional areas. In this chapter we will examine best
practices in forecasting, the methods available to the forecaster and analytic
tools that can be used across forecasting methodologies.

Four distinct steps are necessary to create a forecast – defining the need for
the forecast, selecting the appropriate methodology, analysing the results, and
presenting the forecast to the end-user. These steps are shown in Figure 2.1
and will be discussed in detail during the remainder of this chapter.

DEFINE THE FORECAST

The first step in the forecasting process is to understand the use to which the
forecast will be directed. Is it for a new product in late stage development?
If so, the forecast may be over a ten-year horizon and constructed to yield
annual revenue results. Is it for a currently marketed product? If so, the
appropriate outputs may need to be at the monthly level, at both revenue
and unit levels, and calculated over a two- to three-year horizon. Is the
forecast one that will be used for business development decisions? If so, the
forecast algorithm may need to evaluate the role of potential development
or marketing partners, or may need to explicitly evaluate the financial terms
of any deal that may be constructed. Is the forecast for a single country or

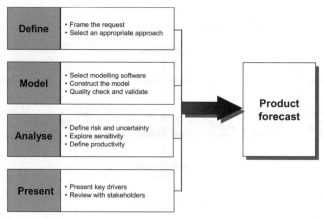

Figure 2.1   The process of forecasting

multiple countries? The answer to this question may govern the choice of methodology and framework used to evaluate a product's forecast potential. Is the forecast for a specific disease state that is treated by pharmaceutical as well as non-pharmaceutical interventions? If so, the forecaster may need to model out non-pharmaceutical or over-the-counter interventions as well as pharmaceutical products. Will the forecast be used to drive financial planning, manufacturing, portfolio investment decisions, compensation schemes, or some combination of these and other uses? As you can well imagine, the list of potential questions can be lengthy, but the answers to these questions govern the selection of methodology and forecast construction.

The widespread use of forecasts in multiple business decisions makes it paramount for the forecaster to understand the role of the forecast when they are constructing the model and analysis. The first step in any forecasting exercise is therefore to meet with the recipients and users of the forecast and to understand the business decisions affected by the forecast. Only after understanding the questions that need to be answered can the forecaster select the appropriate methodology and analytics.

Balance points in forecasting

As discussed in Chapter 1, the forecaster often is confronted with balancing the demands of multiple stakeholders and functional groups. This chapter presents another set of balance challenges to the forecaster – that of methods and process in forecasting. This balance point – often overlooked – also may be stated as the balance between 'breadth' and 'depth', or the balance between a *process* or a *technical* focus. This is illustrated in Figure 2.2. To illustrate the difference, let's consider the two extreme points – a forecast that is overly weighted on process versus one overly weighted on the technical side.

A process focus to forecasting implies that organisational 'buy-in' to the forecast is a key requirement. The forecast must be able to be widely disseminated and understood within the organisation. More importantly, the

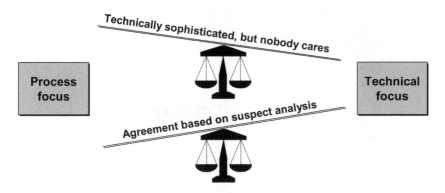

Figure 2.2   Forecasting is a balancing act

end users agree to and support the forecast. Sometimes this can compromise the technical sophistication of the forecast. If it needs to be accepted by a broad base of users – for example, manufacturing, marketing and management – the model may be packaged in a way that makes the numbers and the underlying calculations very transparent and easily digested; this may involve sacrificing some of the technical rigour. In an organisation that is too heavily process-focused the users agree to the result, but often it may well be based on superficial analytics, suspect analysis, or sophistry.

In the other extreme – that of too technical a focus – the forecast construct tends to be very complex. The model may consist of multiple pages in a workbook, have numerous input variables, and employ state-of-the-art risk and uncertainty analyse. Typically these models, because of the complexity involved, have a 'black box' feeling about them: the casual user cannot dissect the analytics or make simple changes to the model. The end user must adopt a trust strategy for the forecast outputs – believing in the results of the forecast model without needing to understand all the steps and calculations involved. Although technically sophisticated, typically these models are not readily agreed to within an organisation. In an organisation that is too technically focused the explanation for a forecast often is 'because the model tells us', which can lead to distrust of or apathy about the results. Organisations that rely heavily on this approach to forecasting are trapped in a technical trench.

Neither of these two extremes is attractive, but unfortunately both occur frequently in organisations. Changing a forecast result to obtain buy-in for the numbers, or deferring to 'the model' when explaining a forecast are all too common phenomena in today's environment. The challenge to the forecaster is to balance the forecasting process such that both extremes are avoided.

Where that balance point exists, however, is more a function of an organisation's culture than it is of forecasting best practices. For example, in a consensus-driven organisation, where buy-in to the forecast is more valued than the technical underpinnings, the forecasting approach is more process oriented. Conversely, in an analysis-driven company, the importance of deep

In an organisation that is too heavily process-focused the users agree to the result, but often it may well be based on superficial analytics, suspect analysis, or sophistry.

THE FORECASTING
PROCESS

technical analysis may be more valued than having all the stakeholders agree to the forecast. To the extent that an organisation's culture focuses exclusively on one end of the balance beam – and ignores the other end – the forecast loses its integrity.

SELECT A FORECAST METHOD

The most dangerous, misused and thought-annihilating piece of technology invented in the past 15 years has to be the electronic spreadsheet. Every day, millions of managers boot up their Lotus 1-2-3s and Microsoft Excels, twiddle a few numbers and diligently sucker themselves into thinking that they're forecasting the future.[1]

This 1991 quote by Michael Schrage is a provocative one. He goes on to say that given his choice, he would rather hire a good science fiction writer than an analytical guru to do forecasting. The point of these sentiments is that forecasting is much more than placing models in a spreadsheet: it is imagining what the future may hold and then communicating that assessment to others.

Although it is doubtful that science fiction writers will replace business analysts in the pharmaceutical industry, the lesson of capturing future scenarios into forecast models is important, and a concept that we will revisit when discussing analytic tools that enhance a forecast model. Many of the elements of Michael Schrage's criticisms are relevant to the pharmaceutical industry, where the ubiquitous tool of choice for forecasting is spreadsheet modelling.

The most dangerous, misused and thought-annihilating piece of technology invented in the past 15 years has to be the electronic spreadsheet.

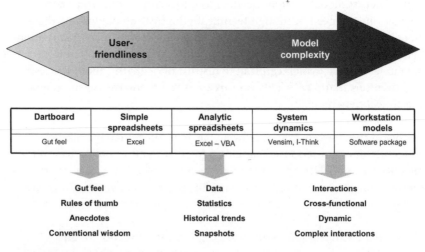

Figure 2.3   Forecast methods

---

1   Schrage, M. (1991) 'Spreadsheets Paper Over Real Problems', *Los Angeles Times*, 11 April, part D, p. 1.

A more comprehensive list of methodologies is illustrated in Figure 2.3. As with the balance between the process and the technical elements or forecasting, there is a similar balance in selecting a forecast methodology. This involves a trade-off between user-friendliness and model complexity. The spectrum presented in Figure 2.3 ranges from the most user-friendly technique (gut feel) to complex software models for forecasting. Let's describe the methods and then discuss how to select an approach for a given forecasting exercise.

Dartboard methods

The dartboard, or gut feel, approach to modelling relies upon an individual's knowledge and experience in creating a forecast. The forecast model may be as simple as the user writing down the forecast. This is a valid technique, and if the experience and gut feel of the forecaster is relevant and accurate this may result in an effective forecast. The user may go through a sophisticated set of analytics and logic in their head, but the result of this technique can be as simple as a pure statement of belief from the forecaster. This is a very user-friendly technique and requires little more than pen and paper and some time to reflect. However, if the thought process used by the forecaster has not been documented adequately the forecast takes on a black box feel due to lack of transparency. Moreover, using the gut feel techniques without documenting and explaining the logic used by the forecaster results in a loss of institutional memory if the forecaster moves on to other responsibilities.

Simple spreadsheets, like those created in Excel, are the dominant method of forecast creation today.

Workstation methods

At the other extreme are workstation models, which typically employ rigorous analytics. These may include statistical time series analysis, longitudinal patient flow modelling, in-depth analogue libraries, or many other techniques. The hallmark of these methods is that the number of datapoints required to be analysed is so numerous, or the forecast flows are so convoluted, that sophisticated software programs are required. In these techniques the user typically enters data into the computer along with assumptions and the model presents output forecasts. As with the too technical focus on forecasting, this too can take on a black box feel, with a methodology and process that are incomprehensible to the average user. Also with these software packages, customisation or changing the algorithm for therapy-specific issues is either impossible, or at the very least, difficult.

Simple spreadsheet methods

Because of the disadvantages of both extremes most organisations use one of the three mid-range methods. Simple spreadsheets, like those created in Excel, are the dominant method of forecast creation today. Most analysts are familiar with spreadsheet software and are comfortable creating formulae to model the market and create forecasts. Most end-users of forecasts are familiar enough with spreadsheet software that they can navigate the model and audit the logic used in forecast creation. Possibly to Michael Schrage's chagrin, this method is the dominant one used today.

Analytic spreadsheet methods

There is a migration of methodology from summary spreadsheets to more complex analytic spreadsheets which usually involve navigational tools (for example, moving from country to country or between patient segments) and analytical functions (such as uncertainty analysis and simulation methodology) built into the spreadsheet model. The typical example of this form of model is an Excel spreadsheet that uses Visual Basic for Applications to run the forecast algorithm and create both chart and tabular outputs. The enhanced sophistication of these models is at the expense of user-friendliness (if changing the model requires the user to make programmatic changes in the Visual Basic set up), but many organisations are now choosing this balance point.

Systems dynamics methods

A more sophisticated method that has emerged in the last decade is that of systems dynamics modelling.[2] In this approach to forecasting the user can create models that track an individual's disease progression over time and can create feedback loops in the forecast model. For example, if a patient cycles between treatment, remission and relapse, systems dynamics models can capture this pattern. Trying to model the same dynamic in a spreadsheet model results in the circular reference error that plagues users of spreadsheets. (Circular reference is a software error that Excel users receive when they reference a value that is used in a calculation. For example, in the equations $A = B$, $B = C$ and $C = A$, $C = A$ would be referred to as a circular reference.) The trade-off to systems dynamics models is that they have a very different look and feel than spreadsheet models and require a degree of training both to create, use, and interpret the results of these platforms. As pharmaceutical modelling moves more into treatment paradigm and disease progression models the systems dynamics approach is gaining support. There are several commercially available software packages that support systems dynamics models, such as iThink, Vensim and Powersim.

Examples of all these modelling platforms are given in subsequent chapters and we will discuss each in more depth. The challenge to the forecaster at this point is to select the method that is aligned with an organisation's culture balance between user-friendliness and technical complexity.

Which of these methods yield the more accurate result? None of them. A forecaster with good experience and insight can create a gut feel forecast that is just as accurate – if not more so – than a sophisticated software package. Which of these methods is more transparent? The ones in the middle. The gut feel methods lack transparency when the logic that is used to develop the forecast is resident only within the forecaster's thoughts and is not documented and explained in the forecast. The workstation models lack

---

2   Paich, M., Peck, C. and Valant, J. (2005) *Pharmaceutical Product Strategy: Using Dynamic Modeling for Effective Brand Planning*, Boca Raton, FL: CRC Press.

transparency when the algorithm and processing of the data are too black box. Which of these methods is more defensible? The ones in the middle, due to their transparency.

Alignment with lifecycles

The choice of forecast method not only depends upon the balance between user-friendliness and model complexity, but also is closely aligned with the lifecycle of a product. Figure 2.4 illustrates a typical lifecycle for a pharmaceutical product, from preclinical research through launch and on to loss of marketing exclusivity.

Earlier we posed the question of whether or not a single forecast model can be used throughout the lifecycle of a product. The answer is no. This is because of a dramatic change in methodology that occurs when a product launches to the market and starts to generate time series data. The launch of a product to market begins the generation of data related to a product's use – prescriptions, days of therapy, pills dispensed and so forth. The advent of data, more specifically time series data, forces a change in forecasting methods from the more qualitative methods to quantitative ones. We will revisit this distinction after we discuss some of the qualitative issues that a forecaster must address in modelling.

Qualitative and quantitative methods

The primary job of the forecaster is to blend qualitative factors into a quantitative framework that creates revenue and unit expectations for a product. This blending is illustrated in Figure 2.5. The quantitative tools – such as sensitivity analysis, probability generation and net present value calculations – are well developed. The more qualitative elements are a challenge. Quantifying the effects of competition, market perception, reimbursement issues, promotional levels, compliance and so forth presents a considerable challenge to the forecaster. These qualitative elements are present in both new product and in-market forecast models, and the forecaster must deal with their quantification in any methodology.

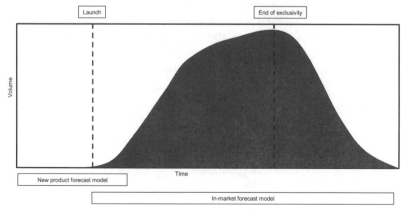

The choice of forecast method not only depends upon the balance between user-friendliness and model complexity, but also is closely aligned with the lifecycle of a product.

Figure 2.4   Alignment of forecast methods with the product lifecycle

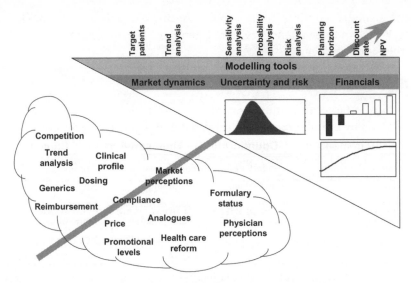

Figure 2.5   Combining qualitative and quantitative methods

How does the forecaster quantify these qualitative elements? Through the use of data and tacit knowledge, as illustrated in Figure 2.6. There are a variety of techniques available to the forecaster to collect data – many of them qualitative in nature as well, but several that also fall into a more quantitative realm. These techniques, when combined with a forecaster's – and/or an organisation's – tacit knowledge, create the quantification needed for forecasting. An example of such a combination is conducting a market research study to collect physician perceptions, and then interpreting the results of these physician responses to create forecast share for a product.

Figure 2.7 presents some of the techniques available to a forecaster for collecting data. The column on the far left – the 'judgement' techniques – is

How does the forecaster quantify these qualitative elements?

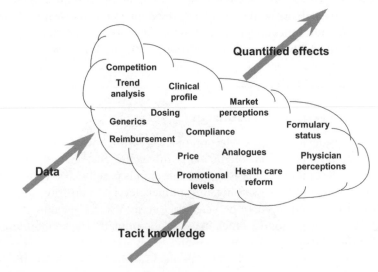

Figure 2.6   The quantification process

- The decision points that require a forecast depend upon the stage of product development

- As the product goes from stage to stage, the forecasting approach also must evolve

Judgement	Counting	Time series	Causal
Historical analogy	Secondary data	Moving average	Correlation
Naive extrapolation	Market research	Smoothing	Regression
Delphi	Conjoint	Adaptive filtering	Leading indicators
Scenario		Decomposition	Input–output
Expert workshop		Trend extrapolation	Econometric
Cross-impact		ARIMA	Autoregression

Figure 2.7   Methods in forecast evolution

purely qualitative. As we move towards the right, the techniques become increasingly quantitative in nature. The techniques in the first two columns are applicable to new product forecasting. Once time series data are available (after a product launches to the market) the tools in the two columns on the right may be applied. As such, these techniques are somewhat aligned with the lifecycle of a product and the evolution of a forecast.

The first set of tools – the judgement tools – are all designed to capture opinions from a subset of respondents. The second set – the counting tools – capture judgements from a larger sample size and then project the responses to a larger universe of decision makers. The time series tools all look at historical data points to determine a trend in the historical data and then project these data into the future. The causal tools look to determine the relationship among historical data elements to determine a cause and effect relationship that can be used to project future data. Detailed definitions for each of these techniques are given in the Appendix. These tools are used both within and outside the pharmaceutical industry. The tools do not operate independently from each other, and frequently several techniques are used together in generating a forecast.

Linking forecasts to resources

One final consideration in the selection of a forecasting method is the resource question: forecasters often refer to this as the 'chicken and egg' question. In new product forecasting the question is posed as 'Do I create a forecast for the product assuming an "optimal" level of marketing and sales resources are deployed, or do I create a forecast using a given level of marketing and sales resource which may be sub-optimal?' The conundrum arises because the determination of resource levels applied to a product is related to the forecast potential for the product ... which also is a function of the level of resources applied against the product. This circular logic is

The conundrum arises because the determination of resource levels applied to a product is related to the forecast potential for the product ... which also is a function of the level of resources applied against the product.

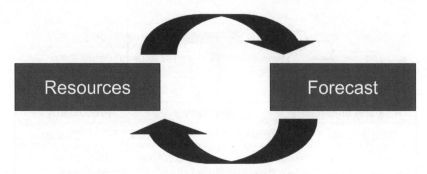

Figure 2.8   The linkage of resources to the forecast

The true goal of the forecaster should be to present these uncertainties, risks and sensitivities to the decision-makers so they can make more informed decisions.

depicted in Figure 2.8 and almost invariably occurs in forecasting. The issue is easier to model in in-market forecasting because of the observed relationship between resources and product performance, but these data are not available for products in development.

There are two approaches by which the forecaster can model this linkage. In the first approach the forecaster defines an optimal level of resources needed for the product to reach its theoretical potential. The forecaster then defines the relationship between the forecast both at optimal and lower resource levels. As the resource levels are lowered the forecast also is lowered according to this defined resource responsiveness. In the second approach the forecaster assumes a 'realistic' level of resources applied against the product and then models both the increase (as resources are raised) and decrease (as resources are lowered) in the product forecast. The two approaches are identical in their analytics – only the starting point for the analysis has changed. As mentioned above, this technique when applied to in-market products is valid; when applied to new products the forecaster is challenged with the need to develop the resource response curve. More challenging, however, is the tendency of organisations to overlook the resource assumptions in the new product forecast. Frequently a new product forecast is 'booked' on the financials several years before the resource assumptions are made, and as the product nears launch and resource allocation decisions are taken the forecast is not adjusted.

ENABLE ANALYTIC INSIGHTS

When asked the question 'What is the goal of forecasting?' a common – in fact the most common – response is 'to accurately forecast the future'. As we saw in Chapter 1, the track record for forecasting accuracy across a number of industries is not good, and we discussed the reasons for this – such as changes in the business environment, assumptions that were biased or that did not bear out in the market, and uncertain data. The true goal of the forecaster should be to present these uncertainties, risks and sensitivities to the decision-makers so they can make more informed decisions.

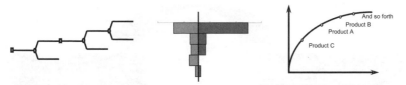

Risk and uncertainty	Sensitivity	Productivity
Simulations	Sensitivity analysis	Net present value
Scenarios	Tornado diagrams	Return on investment
Decision analysis	Waterfall diagrams	Break-even analysis
		Risk versus return
		Productivity multiple

Figure 2.9   Analytic tools in forecasting

There are a number of analytic tools that can be used to obtain additional insights from forecasting models and these are represented in Figure 2.9. Risk and uncertainty analysis allow the user to better understand both the upside potential and downside risk to the forecast. Sensitivity analysis maps the connections between input variables and forecast outputs, educating the user to those input variables that most dramatically affect the forecast outcome. Productivity measures enable the recipients of multiple forecasts to compare the financial value of products and projects to the organisation.

Risk and uncertainty

Risk and uncertainty are concepts frequently used interchangeably when discussing product forecasts. For many people the difference between 'What is the risk of the product not launching?' and 'What is the uncertainty of the product launching?' is inconsequential. Similarly, questions such as 'What is the risk that we will not achieve our sales forecast?' and 'How certain are you that we will achieve our sales forecast?' are viewed as synonymous. In fact, the concepts of risk and uncertainty represent two very different dynamics in the marketplace and should be treated differently. Before discussing the analytic tools available for risk and uncertainty analysis we need to discuss the definitions of these concepts.

From the forecaster's perspective the difference between risk and uncertainty is related to if (and when) the uncertainty is resolved.

From the forecaster's perspective the difference between risk and uncertainty is related to if (and when) the uncertainty is resolved. Risk is resolved throughout the planning process as a product progresses in its development; uncertainty remains even after the product launches to the market. For example, the risk of not launching can be quantified by determining the probability of launch, defined as the probability of achieving each clinical milestone in the development path. Even after a product launches, however, there remains uncertainty in the forecast related to uncertainty in the input assumptions. This uncertainty is inherent in the forecast itself, because of uncertainty in input assumptions. For example, in a forecast for congestive heart failure the sources of prevalence for the disease may range between

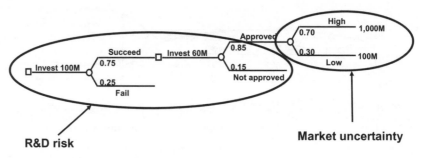

Figure 2.10   Risk and uncertainty

1 and 3 per cent of the population. Assuming a critical review of the data cannot resolve the differences in prevalence rates, what data should the forecaster use? If the forecaster uses either pure data source there will be a threefold difference in the size of the potential patient pool. If the forecaster combines the two datapoints to average out 2 per cent and uses this as the forecast they will be either overestimating (if 1 per cent is the accurate number) or underestimating (if 3 per cent is the accurate number) the forecast potential. In this simple example, exclusively using any of the three potential measures – 1, 2, or 3 per cent – leads to an inaccurate portrayal of the potential patients. A more informed forecast would show the range of outcomes associated with the range of valid input assumptions.

These concepts are presented in Figure 2.10. In this simple illustration, risk – specifically R&D risk – is represented by the probability of a successful clinical outcome and the probability of achieving approval (product registration) by the regulatory authorities. Once the product is launched to the market, there still exists uncertainty around the forecast – represented by a high and low forecast potential. These two potential outcomes may represent the forecast

A more informed forecast would show the range of outcomes associated with the range of valid input assumptions.

High
0.70   1,000M
Approved
0.85   0.30 ———— 100M
Succeed   Invest 60M   Low
0.75
Invest 100M   0.15
0.25   Not approved
Fail

R&D risk   **Market uncertainty**

R&D risk as a probability of launch

= Probability of clinical success x probability of approval

= 0.75 x 0.85

= 0.64

= 64%

Figure 2.11   Calculating risk as a probability of launch

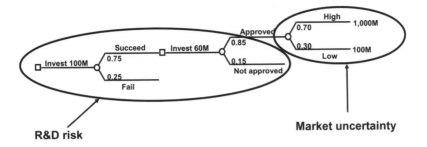

R&D risk

Market uncertainty

Uncertainty in the expected commercial value

= Probability of low revenue multiplied by the low revenue

+ probability of high revenue multiplied by the high revenue

= (0.30 x 100M) + (0.70 x 1,000M)

= 730M

Figure 2.12   Uncertainty as an expected value

associated with different patient pool numbers, compliance rates and any combination of other input variables where uncertainty remains.

The analytical approaches to modelling risk and uncertainty vary. Because risk is resolved as development proceeds we can model it using simple decision trees, where the probability at each node in the decision tree is combined to yield an overall risk factor. This 'probability of launch' factor for the above example is shown in Figure 2.11.

Uncertainty remains in the forecast even after product launch. In its simplest analytic form we can translate the uncertainty in the revenue stream into an expected value of the revenue. This is done by taking each discrete outcome and weighting it by the probability of occurrence. In our simple example above this leads to the expected value shown in Figure 2.12.

Simulations

There are more insights to be gained, however, by considering a continuous distribution of forecast uncertainty, instead of the discrete end points presented in the decision tree example. An example of this is shown in Figure 2.13. Traditional views of forecasting posit uncertainty as a negative outcome of forecasts, arguing that the greater the uncertainty in a forecast the less accurate the forecast. This is a rather myopic view of forecasting because there is a tremendous amount of valuable information in the drivers of forecast uncertainty. For example, consider the distribution of potential forecast outcomes as shown in Figure 2.13. (We will discuss how this distribution is generated in the next section.) By understanding the potential forecast outcomes, and the probability associated with the outcomes, recipients of the forecast can make a more informed judgement as to which outcome to use for planning purposes.

There is a tremendous amount of valuable information in the drivers of forecast uncertainty.

THE FORECASTING PROCESS

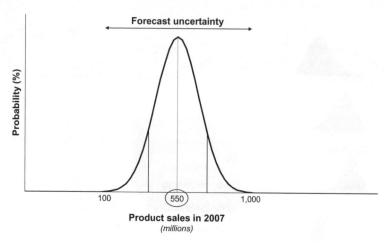

Figure 2.13 Uncertainty as a range of potential outcomes

There are multiple strategic and tactical plans drawn from a single forecast range, where the tolerance in the planning function links to the probability of the forecast outcome.

The linkage of informed planning to forecast uncertainty is shown in Figure 2.14. In this example the full range of potential forecast outcomes is shown. The various planning functions can then draw from within this range for planning purposes. For manufacturing, a forecast above the midpoint may be drawn to allow for overstocking in order to avoid out-of-product situations. The compensation plan for the field sales organisation may be drawn from a slightly increased forecast from the most likely value to allow for 'stretch goals' in the incentive compensation scheme. Financial planners may draw from below the most likely value if they are doing contingency planning for low probability – but high financial effect – scenarios. In essence, each planning function can draw from within the range of expected outputs according to the needs of the forecast. This avoids the need for multiple, and different, forecasts circulating within an organisation. Instead there are multiple strategic and tactical plans drawn from a single forecast range, where the tolerance in the planning function links to the probability of the forecast outcome.

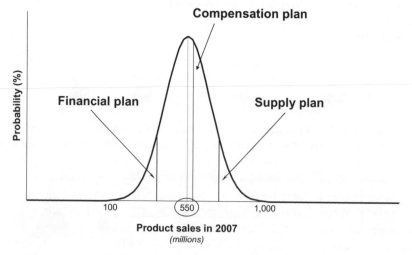

Figure 2.14 Linking planning to forecast uncertainty

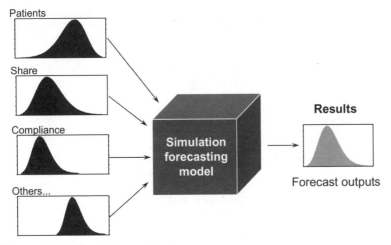

Figure 2.15 Simulation methods

Generating ranges of forecast outcomes is accomplished using simulation methodology. Simulation methods combine the uncertainty of the input variables to create a distribution of outputs, as shown in Figure 2.15. The core of this method is to run the forecast algorithm multiple times, each time drawing a point value randomly from the distribution of each input variable. As the number of independent runs increases, the distribution of outputs occurs (one output associated with each iteration of the forecast algorithm), as shown in Figure 2.16. The skewness of the input ranges, if any, is preserved and transferred into the output range. These methods effectively capture the uncertainties inherent in the input assumptions and translate these uncertainties into the forecast outputs. There are software tools that enable the user to perform these simulations. Programs such as Crystal Ball, At Risk and Risk Detective all are Excel add-in programs that create this capability. It also is possible to enable Excel to perform these calculations without using additional software by using Visual Basic for Applications within Excel itself. Typically several hundred iterations are required to produce a well-distributed outcome.

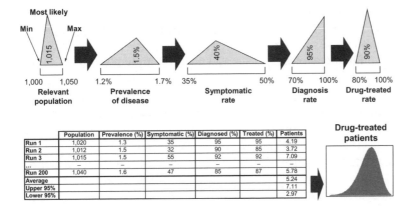

Figure 2.16 Simulation methods generate output ranges

Generating ranges of forecast outcomes is accomplished using simulation methodology.

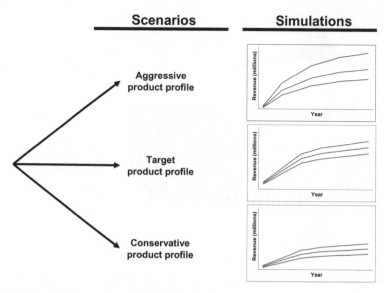

Figure 2.17 Scenario and simulation techniques

Scenarios

Simulation methods are appropriate for most input variables that range in the forecast. There are, however, some input variables that create strong dependencies on the other variables in the forecast. When strong dependency exists simulation methods are not appropriate; in this case the forecaster must use discrete scenarios. Examples of variables for which scenario – instead of simulation – methods are employed are product profiles, launch date and price. Each of these example variables is strongly linked to other variables in the forecast. The product profile assumption may drive share, drug treatment rate, compliance, price and so forth. Likewise, launch date may drive adoption, peak share, price and reimbursement. For these variables a forecaster employs scenario analysis. This is depicted in Figure 2.17.

When strong dependency exists simulation methods are not appropriate; in this case the forecaster must use discrete scenarios.

The example in Figure 2.17 applies to scenarios of three product profiles, each of which generates forecasts using simulation methods across the remaining input variables. The user defines a discrete scenario, such as 'aggressive product profile', and then determines the ranges of the other input variables that depend on this defined profile. The forecast output range is generated simulating across the variables for the defined scenario. If there are three scenarios – in this example, three product profiles – there are three distinct forecast outputs, each of which is ranged through simulation across the other inputs. If there are multiple variables that require discrete scenarios, the number of combinations rapidly increases. For example, three product profiles combined with three price points can create up to nine discrete scenarios. The forecaster must decide which of these scenarios needs to be further evaluated using simulation techniques.

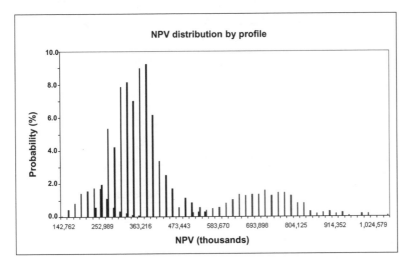

Figure 2.18 Combining scenarios and simulations for portfolio planning

At this point a forecast used for portfolio planning purposes diverges from a forecast used for most other planning purposes. For tactical planning – marketing, operations and so forth – the 'most likely' forecast is used. Ranges around the most likely forecast will have been created from simulation around the input variable ranges. For portfolio planning purposes (where the trade-offs being discussed are across products in development) a 'probabilised' forecast is used. The probabilised forecast takes into account all of the discrete scenarios, not just the 'most likely' scenario. In the example using three product profiles, each scenario would be assigned a probability of occurrence. The sum of all the probabilities adds to 100 per cent. The outputs are then weighted by this assigned probability to yield an aggregate, probabilised revenue or net present value. An example of this is given in Figure 2.18.

What is the danger of confusing scenarios and simulations? If scenario variables such as product profile, launch date or price are included in forecast simulations there exists the possibility of nonsensical combinations, for example, a conservative target product profile linked with high share and rapid adoption, or a high price linked to rapid adoption with no time for reimbursement negotiations. While these may indeed be plausible scenarios it falls to the forecaster to ensure that these are conscious choices and not simply artefacts of the simulation methodology.

Decision analysis

Combining risk and uncertainty analytics opens the door to decision analysis, which is used in strategic planning. Although outside the scope of this book it is important to recognise the role of forecasting in decision analysis. If we consider a typical decision analysis framework (a simplified version is shown in Figure 2.19) the value of each node in the decision tree is ultimately dependent upon the revenue forecast. If the forecast is not rigorous and errors

Combining risk and uncertainty analytics opens the door to decision analysis, which is used in strategic planning.

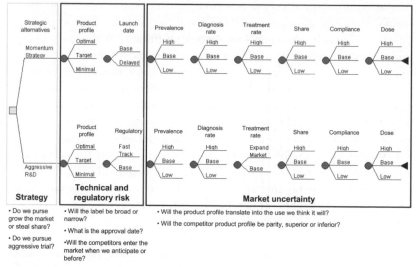

Figure 2.19   Decision analysis framework

propagate back through the decision tree, the strategic direction of R&D programmes and the organisation itself may be affected.

Sensitivity analytics

Ranged forecast outputs also have the advantage that they enable sensitivity analysis. The goal of sensitivity analysis is to link the input assumptions to the outputs, determining the degree to which the forecast outputs depend on each input variable. To a first approximation, the forecast is said to be most sensitive to the input variable that most affects the outputs.

Tornado diagrams

The classic method for sensitivity analysis is the Tornado diagram, as shown in Figure 2.20. Tornado diagrams – so named because they are shaped like

Variable	Most likely value	Effect of variable range on outcome
Patient pool (millions)	80	60 / 120
Marketing costs (thousands)	2,752	3,375 / 2,250
Peak patient share	39%	30% / 50%
Dose per day (mg)	60	30 / 60
COGS per kilo	10,200	12,750 / 7,500
Phase IV Costs (thousands)	70.2	85.5 / 57.5
Capital spend (millions)	70	85 / 65
Sales force costs (thousands)	32.4	38.2 / 25.0
Development costs (millions)	50.1	53.0 / 43.0

↑

Most likely values

Figure 2.20   Tornado diagram

a funnel – capture the effect of each input variable on the forecast. In this example, the range associated with the first listed variable – patient pool – affects the forecast outcome by the largest magnitude. At the 'most likely' value of 80 million patients the forecast would be 750 million in value (in this example we use net income as the value indicator, however revenue also may be used in Tornado diagrams). If the patient pool were only 60 million the forecast drops to approximately 300 million in net income. At the high patient pool value of 120 million, the forecast net income would be approximately 1,750 million. To obtain these net income values locate the low, most likely and high values on the bar representing the patient pool and read the net income from the scale above. Note that all the most likely values for each input variable are aligned in the centre of the diagram (which corresponds to 750 million in net income). This is the central axis upon which all the input bar ranges are based.

This diagram is very powerful in communicating forecast sensitivities. Simple inspection of the example diagram lets the reviewer know that the forecast output is most sensitive to the range associated with the patient pool and least sensitive to the range associated with development costs.

An added benefit of Tornado diagrams is their ability to be used as a strategic planning tool. By examining the list of input variables and the magnitude of the forecast change associated with each input, the strategic planner can focus their efforts on the variables most likely to respond to company strategies. In the example we are using, focusing strategies on increasing the patient pool potentially could yield a greater return on investment than strategies targeted at increasing peak patient share. This is because the upside potential from an increase in the patient pool is greater than the upside potential from an increase in share. Analogously, decreasing the capital spending will not affect the forecast as much as decreasing the cost of goods sold (COGS). Some companies assign coefficients of affectability to each of the input variables to direct marketing strategies towards those variables that can be most influenced. These coefficients of affectability typically range from zero to one, where zero implies that no strategies or actions of the marketing organisation can affect the uncertainty associated with the output, and a value of one implies that the uncertainty can be totally controlled by marketing actions.

Waterfall diagrams

Waterfall diagrams provide a second set of sensitivity measures in the forecast (an example is given in Figure 2.21). Waterfall diagrams (so named because of the cascading set of bars in the diagram) present the effect of the variables used to modify the patient pool. Reading from left to right we can follow the patients from the total prevalent patients (13,560,000 in this example) to the number of patients who are eligible for prescription drug therapy (1,222,000). Examining the diagram gives the user insights into which filters are responsible for drops in the number of eligible patients – that is, the sensitivity of the patient pool to the various forecast filters. Analogous to the use of Tornado diagrams, these insights can be turned into strategic actions by

Waterfall diagrams (so named because of the cascading set of bars in the diagram) present the effect of the variables used to modify the patient pool.

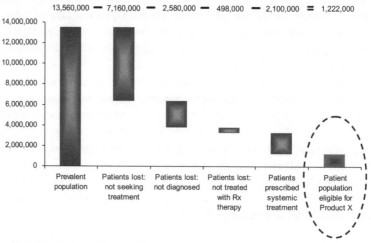

13,560,000 ▬ 7,160,000 ▬ 2,580,000 ▬ 498,000 ▬ 2,100,000 ▬ 1,222,000

Figure 2.21   Waterfall diagram

focusing marketing efforts on those variables that most affect the patient flow. In the example given in Figure 2.21, focusing on increasing the percentage of patients seeking treatment potentially would yield greater growth than focusing on percentage of patients treated with Rx therapy.

Productivity

The final set of forecast analytics focus on productivity measures, defined as a set of financial outputs and ratios. The outputs listed in Figure 2.9 in the Productivity column (that is, NPV, return on investment, break-even analysis, risk versus return and the productivity multiple) are standard financial measures. One measure that is gaining increased use is the productivity multiple. An example of the calculation of the productivity multiple is given in Figure 2.22. We have discussed the calculations for R&D risk and expected commercial value in prior sections. The expected development cost is calculated in a similar manner as the expected commercial value, weighting the investments required by the probability of progress along the decision

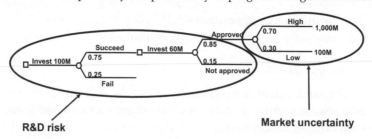

R&D risk as a probability of launch = 0.75 x 0.85 = 0.64 = 64%

Expected commercial value = (0.70 x 1,000M) + (0.30 x 100M) = 730M

Expected development cost = (1.00 x 100M) + (0.75 x 60M) = 145M

Productivity multiple = (730M / 145M) x 0.64 = 3.2

Figure 2.22   Calculation of the productivity multiple

tree. The productivity multiple is defined as the expected commercial value divided by the expected development cost; then weighted by the probability of launch. For the example in Figure 2.22 this results in a productivity multiple of 3.2.

The productivity multiple is a valid measure to apply in cross-product or cross-project comparisons. A preliminary comparison of two products (or projects) would suggest that the product with the higher productivity multiple might be a better investment for an organisation because the expected return on investment to the company would be larger. This is one of the first steps in R&D portfolio comparisons.

PRESENT THE RESULTS

In the mid 1960s, a group of 'visionaries' united to form the nucleus of futurology, or the rational study of the future.

In the mid 1960s, a group of 'visionaries' united to form the nucleus of futurology, or the rational study of the future. These self-named futurists insist on a rational and pragmatic approach to discussing the future. Rather than claiming to forecast the future through mystical predictions they focus on creating models, or frameworks, in which to discuss potential future outcomes. Their organisation – the World Future Society – has examined forecasts across a number of different industries, and has created a list of lessons learned in presenting forecasts.[3] These are summarised in Figure 2.23.

Many of the lessons are obvious and self-explanatory: however, there are three in particular that are common – and often overlooked – in the pharmaceutical industry. The three that warrant further discussion are: 'garbage in, gospel out'; 'beware of the recent past' and 'beware of technological hype'.

'Garbage in, gospel out' is a variation of the more common saying 'garbage in, garbage out'. It is not difficult to believe that when the input assumptions are faulty and ill formed, the forecast will be of low quality – garbage in, garbage out. However, there is a tendency to believe that if the model is complex, if

- **The future is not preordained.**
- **No single method is best in all situations.**
- **Garbage in, gospel out.**
- **Be selective.**
- **Focus on the underlying logic.**
- **A forecast is only as good as its underlying assumptions.**
- **Use ranges or scenarios.**
- **Beware of the recent past.**
- **Beware of technological hype.**
- **Keep asking yourself 'So what?'**

Figure 2.23   Lessons learned in presenting forecasts

---

3   Amara, R. (1989) 'A Note on What We Have Learned About the Methods of Futures Planning', *Technological Forecasting and Social Change*, 36, 43–7.

it has detailed outputs, if there are fancy graphs and (most commonly) if the model cost a lot to build, then it must be good. The user can become lulled into a false sense of confidence in the outputs because of the sophistication of the forecast model itself. In reality, the quality of the forecast remains a function of the quality of the inputs – no matter how sophisticated the forecast model and resulting outputs appear. The lesson of garbage in, gospel out is to avoid the belief that the forecast is better simply because of the sophistication of the model.

'Beware of the recent past' reflects the fact that events that have occurred recently are more in our mind than events that have occurred in the more distant past. This psychology is evident in many areas, but can be of particular concern when forecasting. This dynamic usually plays out in the following scenario. A forecaster is working on a 12-month forecast for a product. The most recent datapoint does not seem to follow the prior 11 months' trend. In reviewing the forecast there is much discussion around this last datapoint – is it a break in the historical trend? Have the results of recent marketing programs started to bear fruit and increase our share (if the recent datapoint is above the trend line)? Are we losing steam in the market or are our competitors doing something that is stealing share from us (if the datapoint is below the trend line)? In reality, the ex-trend datapoint may simply be a data anomaly, or the data may be within the error of the trending methodology. Simply because the information is new, and not part of the historical trend, a reviewer will put more emphasis on the data than a longer-term perspective would dictate. Any forecaster who has had to dampen recent datapoints when trending, or a forecaster who has had to analyse weekly prescription data (as opposed to monthly data) is subject to the recent past bias discussed here.

The third lesson learned that is common in the pharmaceutical industry is 'beware of technological hype'. In academic business courses this is referred to as the 'better mousetrap syndrome'. The lesson discussed in the better mousetrap example is that, while it is certainly possible to design a better mousetrap, the new technology may not generate any additional demand in the marketplace. In the pharmaceutical industry the better mousetrap is often disguised as a novel mechanism of action for drugs in development. Simply because the mechanism of action is different does not guarantee that it will be a better product in the market; however, the bias seen in pharmaceutical forecasting is to over-forecast products with new mechanisms of action. This bias also plays out significantly in market research results, and we will address this in the next chapter.

These three examples arise because of subtle, sometimes unrecognised, bias in how the forecasts are constructed or presented. In presenting any results, the forecaster must also be aware of the more evident biases in the reviewing audience. These biases are reflective of the multiple key stakeholders in forecasting, as discussed in Chapter 1. Each of these stakeholders carries a bias towards the forecast that affects their ability to receive forecast results objectively.

Although these biases can create pressure in presenting forecast results, the fact that the bias is evident makes it easier to address than the more hidden ones discussed above. By incorporating the other lessons learned from Figure 2.23 (focus on underlying logic, use ranges or scenarios and so forth) the forecaster can either rebut any pressures to change the forecast, or can capture the pressure to change in alternative scenarios or within a potential range of outputs. Many readers at this point with think 'easier said than done', and we do not mean to trivialise the difficulty of dealing with pressure to alter the forecast, but it is the job of the forecaster to prepare the best case possible for senior review, to present the logic used in the forecast, and to dissuade – or at a minimum acknowledge – obvious bias when introduced to change the forecast.

It is the job of the forecaster to prepare the best case possible for senior review, to present the logic used in the forecast, and to dissuade – or at a minimum acknowledge – obvious bias when introduced to change the forecast.

FINAL CONSIDERATIONS

This chapter presented the forecasting process for products in the pharmaceutical industry. As we have seen, there are numerous tools that may be employed in forecasting. There are also pitfalls along the way that the forecaster needs to avoid. In the following chapters we will discuss the integration of these concepts into algorithms that may be used for new product and in-market pharmaceutical forecasting.

CHAPTER 3

New Product Forecasting

If a man gives no thought about what is distant he will find sorrow near at hand.

Confucius

A fact poorly observed is more treacherous than faulty reasoning.

Paul Valery

Chapter 2 discussed the alignment of forecasting methodologies with a product's position in its lifecycle. New product forecasting covers the evaluation of a product that is still in development (that is, prior to the product's launch in the marketplace). This chapter presents the process, tools, methods, and algorithms used in new product forecasting.

New product forecasting covers the evaluation of a product that is still in development (that is, prior to the product's launch in the marketplace).

TOOLS AND METHODS

In Chapter 2 we discussed the tools and methods applicable for product forecasting, and identified the judgement-rich methods as those most applicable to new product forecasting. These tools are represented by the 'Judgement' and 'Counting' columns in Figure 2.7.

NEW PRODUCT FORECAST ALGORITHM

The general forecast algorithm used in new product forecasting is presented in Figure 3.1. This algorithm, or simple variations thereof, can be generalised to almost all new product forecasting exercises. The level of detail varies as the forecast needs become more complex, but the same logic flow applies at all points in a product's lifecycle.

The algorithm can be divided into three components (Figure 3.2), representing the elements required to model the market, to forecast the

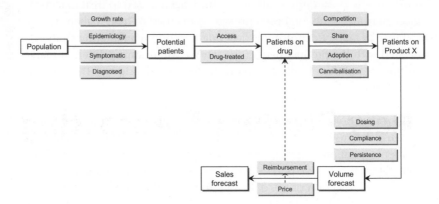

Figure 3.1 Generalised new product forecast algorithm

*Modelling
the market
determines the
potential market
size for new
products.*

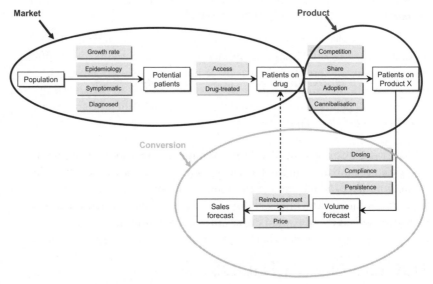

Figure 3.2 Components of the new product forecast algorithm

product, and to convert patients on product into revenue. These structural divisions – market, product, and conversion – form the logical division of market dynamics in new product forecasting.

MODELLING THE MARKET

Modelling the market determines the potential market size for new products. It is a measure of potential and represents the theoretical maximum use for a product. Each market is defined by the user depending upon the dynamics to be forecast in the market. In the simplest example, the forecaster defines the market as those products that compete against each other in the prescription drug market for a specific disease state. Alternatively, this definition can be expanded to include over-the-counter, alternative medicine interventions and diet and exercise regimens. Within a given disease state the market may be defined broadly (for example, all prescription agents used to treat diabetes) or more narrowly (only oral prescription agents used to treat diabetes). The choice of market definition is dependent upon the marketing strategy associated with the product being forecast. We will examine different market definitions – and their implications on the forecast algorithm – throughout this chapter.

Similar to the choice of market definitions, there also is the choice of the underlying data used in modelling out market potential. Should the forecaster use patients, total prescriptions, new prescriptions, days of therapy, revenue, or some other measure of potential use? Analogous to the choice of market definition, the selection of the data used to model the market is a function of the questions being posed to the forecaster. This chapter also will discuss the various data options open to the forecaster in new product forecasting.

Patient versus prescription models

One of the first decisions a forecaster faces is the choice of data used in modelling the market. Should the model be based on patients, prescriptions, days of therapy or some other measure of potential? As with almost all forecasting questions, there is no right or wrong answer to this question. The answer depends upon the goal of the forecast, the therapy area being modelled and the availability of data.

Consider two examples – a patient-based approach and a prescription-based approach, as shown in Figure 3.3. The patient-based modeller starts at the outside of the circle, identifying the number of potential patients with a given disease state, and then contracts the potential patients through a series of filters to arrive at those patients who are receiving drug therapy at this time. The prescription-based modeller starts with the number of patients currently receiving therapy (that is, currently receiving prescriptions) and then expands this number to reach the theoretical maximum. Both approaches yield the same information – it is simply a question of the direction of the analysis.

One of the first decisions a forecaster faces is the choice of data used in modelling the market.

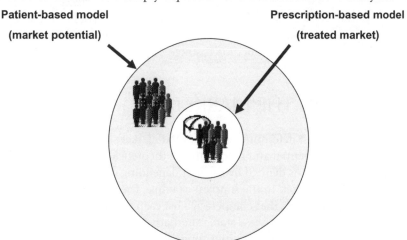

Patient-based model
(market potential)

Prescription-based model
(treated market)

Figure 3.3   Patient- versus prescription-based models

The patient-based algorithm

Consider the patient-based algorithm. In this approach we first define the theoretical maximum number of patients with a given disease state and then contract, or filter, the market to arrive at the number of patients who currently are receiving therapy. This is done through a series of filters, as shown in Figure 3.4. The steps involved in filtering from population for a country or region to patients receiving drug therapy are:

- a measure of disease prevalence or incidence;
- an estimate of the number of patients who are symptomatic for the disease;
- an estimate of the number of patients who are diagnosed correctly with the disease;
- an estimate of the number of patients who have access to health care; and
- an estimate of the number of patients who are treated with drug therapy.

This approach has various names in practice – patient filtering, the health care transaction model, patient intervention models and so forth. Regardless of the name applied, each model determines the difference between the theoretical number of patients and those patients who currently are receiving therapy.

Typically population data are available from a country's census office and are projected over time. Dynamics such as an ageing population, changes in birth or death rates and demographics associated with race and gender are captured in the new product forecast algorithm at this point. (Segmentation will be discussed in a subsequent section of this chapter.)

Each model determines the difference between the theoretical number of patients and those patients who currently are receiving therapy.

Epidemiology data – either prevalence or incidence data – are then applied to the population, or relevant population segment, to determine the number of people with a given disease. (An example of this and subsequent calculations in this section is shown in Table 3.1.) The next steps in the algorithm are to

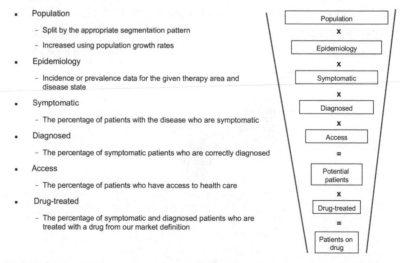

- Population
  - Split by the appropriate segmentation pattern
  - Increased using population growth rates
- Epidemiology
  - Incidence or prevalence data for the given therapy area and disease state
- Symptomatic
  - The percentage of patients with the disease who are symptomatic
- Diagnosed
  - The percentage of symptomatic patients who are correctly diagnosed
- Access
  - The percentage of patients who have access to health care
- Drug-treated
  - The percentage of symptomatic and diagnosed patients who are treated with a drug from our market definition

Population
x
Epidemiology
x
Symptomatic
x
Diagnosed
x
Access
=
Potential patients
x
Drug-treated
=
Patients on drug

Figure 3.4   Filters used to convert potential patients into treated patients

estimate how many of these individuals actually express symptoms for the disease and are correctly diagnosed. If these percentages are less than 100 per cent, then the potential patient pool subsequently contracts. Note in the example in Table 3.1 that the various filter percentages are changing for the two time points in the illustration. Changes in the input assumptions over time is the approach to modelling market growth (or contraction).

Table 3.1   An example of patient-flow forecast calculations (data are illustrative only and are rounded)

Variable name	Variable definition	Value in 2006	Value in 2008
Population (millions)	Number of individuals over age 65 in the United States (in millions)	50.00	55.00
Epidemiology (prevalence)	Percentage of people over age 65 who have rheumatoid arthritis	1%	1%
Prevalent population (millions)	Number of individuals who have the disease (multiplication of population and prevalence percentage)	5.00	5.50
Symptomatic rate	Percentage of prevalent population who exhibit symptoms of the disease	95%	95%
Symptomatic population (millions)	Number of prevalent population who exhibit symptoms of the disease (multiplication of prevalent population and the symptomatic rate)	4.75	5.23
Diagnosis rate	Percentage of symptomatic patients who are properly diagnosed with the disease	90%	95%
Diagnosed population (millions)	Number of symptomatic patients who are properly diagnosed with the disease (multiplication of symptomatic population and the diagnosis rate)	4.28	4.96
Access rate	Percentage of diagnosed patients who have access to or can afford health care	85%	90%

Changes in the input assumptions over time is the approach to modelling market growth (or contraction).

NEW PRODUCT FORECASTING

Table 3.1   *Continued*

*The net result
of applying
these filters is
to convert the
population of a
given geography
into the patients
who currently
are receiving
prescription
drug therapy
in that same
geography. .*

Potential patients (millions)	Number of patients who can potentially be treated for the disease (multiplication of diagnosed population and access rate)	3.63	4.47
Drug treatment rate	Percentage of potential patients who are treated with prescription drug therapy (as opposed to other interventions)	80%	85%
Drug-treated patients (millions)	Number of potential patients who receive prescription drug therapy (multiplication of potential patients by the drug treatment rate)	2.91	3.80

The next filter applied is to correct for the number of patients who have access to health care. In countries where health care is available to all citizens through a national health care system this value can approach 100 per cent. In countries like the United States this value may reflect removal of the uninsured population who do not have access to any private or government health care programmes. For therapy areas where the product is not reimbursed through government or private insurance schemes, this variable may be used to correct for the socio-economics of private purchase of the drug therapy – for example, lifestyle products that are not reimbursed and are priced at levels that exclude the lower socio-economic groups.

The final filter applied represents the percentage of potential patients (patients with the disease who are symptomatic, correctly diagnosed and have access to health care) who choose a prescription drug therapy over a non-drug or non-prescription treatment. As discussed earlier, the definition of drug-treated here is dependent upon the therapy area and the nature of the forecast being requested. Examples include modelling prescription-only treatments, modelling prescription and over-the-counter treatments, modelling alternative medicine and so forth.

The net result of applying these filters is to convert the population of a given geography into the patients who currently are receiving prescription drug therapy in that same geography. Epidemiology data typically are some number less than 100 per cent; however, the other filters can approach 100 per cent. If this is the case then there is little filtering occurring in the market and the number of patients who receive drug therapy is close to the number of patients with a disease. If, however, any of the filters are at values less than

100 per cent this represents growth opportunities in the market. Strategies that increase the flow through of patients (that is, increase the percentage applied in each of the filters) result in market expansion. We will revisit this concept when we discuss the roles of physician medical education and direct-to-consumer strategies.

The prescription-based algorithm

The above discussion applies to the patient-based forecaster, but what of the person who chooses to model the market potential based on prescription data? This individual effectively starts at the centre of the circle in Figure 3.3 and moves to the outside, or to the theoretical maximum. In essence, the forecaster still needs to consider the same filters discussed previously, but the forecaster is looking for the values that allow the current drug-treated patient pool to expand, rather than contract. The only way to expand the market is to identify those variables that can change the universe of currently treated patients and to then grow those variables over time. Once the number of patients with a given disease has been exhausted market expansion must stop – effectively, the forecaster has reached the outer boundary of the circle in Figure 3.3.

Comparison of the two approaches

Which method is preferred? The patient-based forecaster argues that the patient-based method is preferred because it allows the user to identify the theoretical maximum for a product and the pressure points along that way that are constricting the market. The prescription-based forecaster argues that current measures of treatment activity (typically audit data) are more accurate than epidemiology data and that symptomatic and diagnosis rates are difficult to obtain. In essence, the prescription-based forecaster argues that the starting point for the forecast (the data related to current drug usage) is a stronger keystone upon which to build the forecast than the epidemiology data.

Which method is more accurate? Neither, and both. In order to validate the approach both forecasters must use the other method's data as well. For the patient-based modeller the integrity of the forecast must be ensured by validating the results from the patient flow against actual observations in the market – the audited prescription data. For the prescription-based forecaster the only way to know when to halt the market expansion is to identify the upper boundary of the forecast – essentially the maximum number of patients. Both forecasters require the same information and use the same algorithm – the only difference is the starting point.

In order to validate the approach both forecasters must use the other method's data as well.

Examples of success and failure

There are success and failure stories associated with each approach. For the patient-based forecaster success stories revolve around diseases such as benign prostatic hypertrophy and HIV. Benign prostatic hypertrophy (BPH) is a disease that affects men, usually in older age. Cadaveric epidemiological studies suggested that the prevalence of BPH was as high as 95 per cent in men over the age of 65. However, the number of men treated for BPH was significantly lower. With the advent of new diagnostic technologies physicians were able to monitor for an enzyme associated with BPH and were able to diagnose patients earlier in their disease. This led to market growth through an increase in diagnosis rates.

A similar story is associated with HIV disease. With the appearance of new diagnostic tools for the HIV virus (specifically the enhanced sensitivity of PCR-based diagnostic tools) patients with lower levels of the HIV virus were identified earlier and were placed on anti-HIV medications. Again, the use of diagnostic tools enabled market expansion.

Changes in the rate of symptom recognition also increase the size of the market. Examples here include self-examination for breast and testicular cancers, education of transient ischaemic events that may lead to stroke, and recognition that persistent heartburn may be a symptom of other gastrointestinal disorders.

Although the discussion above has been restricted to two examples – patient-based and prescription-based models – similar logic applies to the use of other databases, such as days of therapy, cycles of treatment and so forth. For acute disease states where there may be multiple treatment opportunities in a single year the forecast may be modelled using treatment episodes instead of patients. An example of this would be a forecast for migraine headache, where each patient may experience multiple migraines in a given year. Each episode represents an opportunity for treatment and must therefore be captured explicitly in the forecast model.

Prevalence versus incidence models

There are two approaches for modelling the epidemiology associated with diseases: prevalence and incidence. These two methods are illustrated in Figure 3.5. In a prevalence-based model the user is concerned with the total number of cases of a disease in a given year. Patient history is not needed. It doesn't matter if the patient is in their first, tenth, or fifteenth year of having the disease because the treatment options do not vary significantly.

There are two approaches for modelling the epidemiology associated with diseases: prevalence and incidence.

In an incidence-based epidemiology model patient history is critical. The choice of drug-treatment options is related to patient history – a 'naive' patient who has just been diagnosed with the disease is treated differently than a patient who has prior treatment experience. If the patient is near the end of their treatment cycle – either through cure, remission, or mortality – the choice of treatment options may differ as well. If a patient progresses through stages of a disease an incidence-based platform may need to be used. If the choice of treatment regimen in a latter stage of the disease is dependent upon the drugs used in an earlier stage, the forecaster must use an incidence-based model.

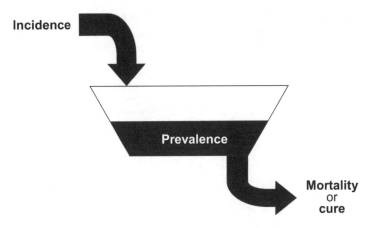

Several therapy
areas require
incidence-
based models:
oncology,
transplantation
and HIV disease.

Figure 3.5   Prevalence- and incidence-based epidemiology

Both types of models are used in forecasting, but prevalence-based platforms are simpler to construct and to use. This is because of the 'accounting' necessary in incidence-based models. The need to keep track of patients on an annual basis and the treatment history associated with each patient cohort adds complexity to the forecast model. For example, consider a forecast over a five-year period for a disease that has two stages. During year five of the forecast model there are ten patient cohorts that need to be accounted for separately, each with potentially different competitive environments, drugs, compliance rates, mortality rates and so forth. Conversely, in a prevalence-based model there would be a maximum of two cohorts – one for each disease stage. In a multi-year, multi-stage disease the complexity of the forecast model can be significant.

When needed, however, incidence-based models can be constructed. Simple incidence-based models can be constructed in spreadsheet software such as Microsoft Excel. For complex models a set of systems dynamics software packages can be used. Several therapy areas require incidence-based models: oncology, transplantation and HIV disease. This requirement occurs because the drug treatment regimen in these disease areas change as a patient progresses through the disease state or treatment options. The choice of subsequent therapies may be dependent upon a patient's response to prior therapy. Increasingly both the central nervous system and cardiovascular disease states are modelled using incidence-based approaches as pharmaceutical companies attempt to model out patient flow at a more detailed level.

Patient-based versus patient-flow models

Figure 3.6 provides an overview of patient-based versus patient-flow models. Patient-based models are best suited for markets where patients can be allocated to different 'buckets' of treatment paradigms, and there is no interdependency between the choice of therapy and progression of disease. Patient-flow models are more dynamic, capturing the time dependencies

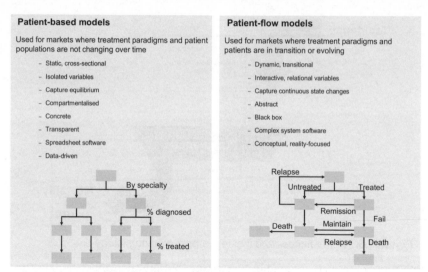

Patient-based models

Used for markets where treatment paradigms and patient populations are not changing over time

- – Static, cross-sectional
- – Isolated variables
- – Capture equilibrium
- – Compartmentalised
- – Concrete
- – Transparent
- – Spreadsheet software
- – Data-driven

By specialty

% diagnosed

% treated

Patient-flow models

Used for markets where treatment paradigms and patients are in transition or evolving

- – Dynamic, transitional
- – Interactive, relational variables
- – Capture continuous state changes
- – Abstract
- – Black box
- – Complex system software
- – Conceptual, reality-focused

Relapse

Untreated   Treated

Remission

Death   Maintain   Fail

Relapse   Death

Figure 3.6   Patient-based and patient-flow models

between patient progression in a given disease state and interdependencies between treatment options. If patients can be allocated to treatment buckets via a simple decision tree analysis, patient-based modelling is appropriate. If, however, patients may cycle between treatment groups, and the choice of therapy may be dependent upon prior treatment history, patient-flow models are most applicable.

Construction of patient-flow models is not possible in linear-thinking programs, such as Excel. In attempting to construct patient-flow models using spreadsheet software the user will receive circular reference errors due to the circular loops encountered in modelling patient movement between disease states or treatment options. Patient-flow models are constructed best in systems dynamics software programs such as iThink, Vensim, or Powersim. An example of a forecast model constructed using a systems dynamics approach is shown in Figure 3.7. (Note that this is a purely illustrative example: readers who wish to pursue patient-flow models in more detail are referred to Paich *et al.* 2005.) The interdependence of treatment options and time-dependence of patient flows in incidence-based therapy areas makes systems dynamics the software of choice when an incidence-based forecast model is required.

Patient segmentation

The approach discussed to date for modelling the market for a product has assumed an undifferentiated patient pool – that is, potential segments of patients have been treated the same in the forecast algorithm. Often this is not a valid assumption and the forecaster needs to divide the patient pool into relevant segments. Examples of common segmentation patterns might be by age, gender, race, severity of the disease, stage of the disease and so forth. Less common – but just as valid – examples of patient segmentation include by specialty of the physician who treats the patient, treatment site, risk-factors, or geography. There are no absolutes in selecting an appropriate

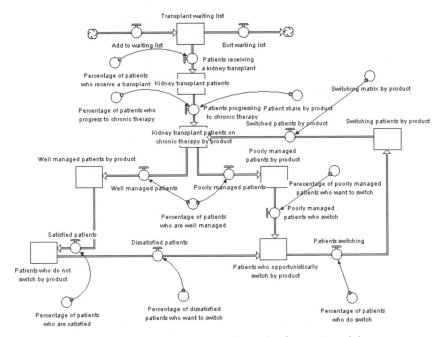

Transplant waiting list

Add to waiting list   Exit waiting list

Patients receiving
a kidney transplant

Percentage of patients
who receive a transplant Kidney transplant patients

Switching matrix by product

Percentage of patients who   Patients progressing Patient share by product
progress to chronic therapy   to chronic therapy
                               Switched patients by product   Switching patients by product

Kidney transplant patients on
chronic therapy by product

Poorly managed
patients by product

Well managed patients by product

Perecentage of poorly managed
patients who want to switch

Well managed patients   Poorly managed patients

Poorly managed
patients who switch

Percentage of patients
who are well managed

Satisfied patients

Dissatisfied patients   Patients switching

Patients who do not
switch by product

Patients who opportunistically
switch by product

Percentage of patients   Percentage of dissatisfied   Percentage of patients
who are satisfied   patients who want to switch   who do switch

Figure 3.7   An example of a systems dynamics forecast model

segmentation pattern; however, the choice of the segments to forecast should
be aligned to the questions and strategies that need to be addressed using the
forecast model.

Once a segmentation pattern is selected the market component of the forecast
algorithm (Figure 3.2) must be modified according to the segmentation
pattern. For example, if the patients are segmented into three age cohorts, the
population used in the forecast flow must also be segmented into the three
age cohorts.

The forecaster must be careful not to be seduced by the lure of too many segments in the forecast model.

This segmentation can be preserved throughout the forecast flow, or the
segments can be combined at any point in the forecast algorithm (see
Figure 3.8). The decision to hold the segmentation pattern throughout
the forecast or to combine segments at various points should be reflective
of the market dynamics as well as the purpose for the forecast. Given the
number of potential segmentation variables and the number of points of
expansion and collapse of segments in the forecast algorithm, it is easy to
envision an almost unlimited set of possibilities for the patient flow. One
of the biggest challenges to the forecaster is to decide on the appropriate
segmentation pattern. Since this is an upstream decision that affects many of
the 'downstream' variables the choice of segmentation is a critical factor in
forecast model design.

The forecaster must be careful not to be seduced by the lure of too many
segments in the forecast model. What can be a very satisfying academic
exercise in creating segments for subpopulations in a therapy area often
turns into a frustrating exercise of collecting data for very targeted (and

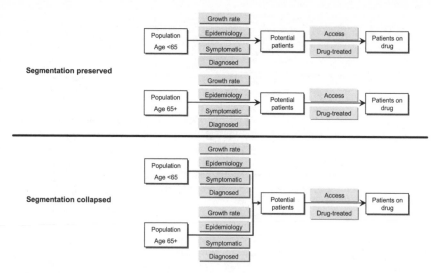

Figure 3.8 Patient segments may be collapsed at any point in the algorithm

small) segments. It is not unusual for a forecaster to create a finely segmented forecast algorithm, only to have to collapse many of the segments when the data are not available for the desired segmentation.

Modelling consumer education effects on the market

Recent years have seen the advent of increasing consumer education efforts, either through the information dissemination by advocacy groups using tools such as the Internet or through direct-to-consumer advertising campaigns in markets such as the United States. The effects of such educational efforts are multifold – affecting variables in all three sections of the new product forecast algorithm (see Figure 3.2). In this section we examine the effects of consumer education in the market.

Consumer education and direct-to-consumer advertising can be modelled using three variables that affect assumptions in the forecast model. These are consumer awareness, consumer intent and consumer action (see Figure 3.9). Consumer awareness acts upon the ability of a patient (and physician) to recognise the symptoms and correctly diagnose a given disease. In theory, educating the patient allows for better self-recognition of disease symptoms and diagnosis (or at least creating awareness that a physician visit for a diagnosis is required). This dynamic – coupled with educating the patient that a drug-therapy is available – is captured in a change in consumer awareness and is translated into increased percentages of symptom recognition and self-diagnosis. In essence, raising the consumer awareness variable increases the market size. The implicit assumption behind product-specific consumer education programmes (that is, direct-to-consumer advertising campaigns) is that this increase in market size will be followed by a direct increase in prescribing behaviour for the product being discussed. We will revisit this assumption when discussing product share projections.

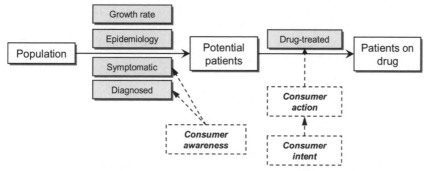

Figure 3.9 The effects of consumer education and direct-to-consumer marketing

There are, however, mitigating variables to increased consumer awareness. The dynamics of consumer intent and consumer action (willingness to act upon that intent) govern changes in the percentage of patients who are treated with drug therapy. Once the consumer is aware of a given disease state they must then visit their physician or health-care provider before a drug can be prescribed. This action of intent to visit a physician, and actual willingness to act upon that intent, govern the changes in the percentage of patients who will receive drug therapy as a result of their heightened awareness. In a perfect scenario, 100 per cent of all consumers who are aware of drug therapy options would visit their physician and receive a prescription. However, in the absence of perfect behaviour (a realistic assumption) the consumer intent and willingness to act upon that intent variables are less than 100 per cent.

Estimating consumer intent and willingness to act upon that intent are significant challenges for the forecaster. There are many well-developed and documented methodologies for measuring consumer awareness, and all of the reputable vendors who perform consumer education and direct-to-consumer advertising campaigns will have historical data that measure the change in consumer awareness. In the case of direct-to-consumer advertising campaigns these measurements are available for all types of advertising media – print, radio, television – and across many types of consumer demographics.

The variables that represent consumer intent and willingness to act upon that intent are more challenging to measure. Typical consumer studies can measure the consumer intent variable by asking the consumer if they indeed will act upon their interest and will visit a physician. How many of these consumers actually follow through on this stated intent and do indeed visit their physician is captured by the consumer action variable. This is not a variable that can be quantified through consumer interviews (where the consumer already has stated their intention). Rather, the measurement on consumer action relies upon monitoring consumer behaviour – how many consumers actually followed through on their intent to visit a physician? The data related to these two variables require monitoring consumer behaviour to gauge the effects of these variables. Whereas there is a wealth of historical information and norms from consumer product research on these values, the

Estimating consumer intent and willingness to act upon that intent are significant challenges for the forecaster.

literature related to physician visits is has a shorter history. The challenge for the forecaster in modelling consumer education effects on the forecast is the challenge in valuing the two variables – consumer intent and consumer action (willingness to act upon that intent).

Concomitancy and polypharmacy

Concomitancy and polypharmacy are two dynamics in the pharmaceutical markets that lead to modification of the basic forecast algorithm for market flow. Concomitancy refers to the use of multiple drugs in the same patient for the same disease state. Polypharmacy refers to the use of multiple drugs in the same patient for different disease states. Of these two events only concomitancy directly affects the calculation of market potential. The effects of polypharmacy occur indirectly on market potential.

The effect of concomitancy is to inflate the number of drug uses for a product compared to the number of patients in the market. Consider a market with 100 patients. If each patient is taking only one drug there are 100 possible drug uses during the treatment period. Consider the same market of 100 patients where 20 of those patients are receiving two drugs instead of one. The total number of possible drug uses is therefore 120 (80 patients receiving 1 drug plus 20 patients receiving 2 drugs). If the product being forecast can be used for the underlying therapy only (that is, as the first drug prescribed) there are 100 possible drug uses. If the product being forecast can be used for the secondary therapy only (that is, as the second drug prescribed) there are 20 possible drug uses. If the product being forecast can be used for either the primary or secondary therapy there are 120 possible drug uses. In a market with concomitant usage the size of the market potential changes depending upon the positioning of the product being forecast. For the forecaster this product positioning question becomes a key driver of forecast structure. Often in a therapy area where concomitant therapy is used and the product being forecast can be used as either the primary or secondary drug, the underlying market is forecast in patient equivalents rather than patients. In the above example, 100 patients would translate into 120 patient equivalents. Concomitant therapy is common in therapy areas such as oncology, diabetes, HIV therapy and central nervous system (CNS) indications such as depression or bipolar disorder.

Concomitancy and polypharmacy are two dynamics in the pharmaceutical markets that lead to modification of the basic forecast algorithm for market flow.

The effects of polypharmacy is indirect on the potential patient calculations. Polypharmacy – also referred to as pill burden – can affect the percentage of patients who seek drug treatment. If a patient has a significant pill burden that translates into a significant cost burden, the patient may elect to forgo drug treatment in an adjunct therapy market. Thus the effect of polypharmacy may be to decrease the percentage of patients who seek drug treatment in a secondary disease state if the pill burden (cost burden) becomes too great.

For example:
The number of patients with unipolar depression is 200,000.
The number of patients with general anxiety disorder is 100,000.
The number of patients with both unipolar depression and general anxiety disorder is 30,000.
What is the number of potential patients for a product that treats both indications?

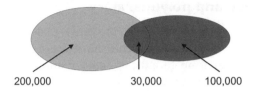

200,000   30,000   100,000

Figure 3.10   The effects of comorbidity on patient pool calculations

A second effect of polypharmacy may be related to fear of drug–drug interactions across the products being used. If the potential for adverse drug–drug interactions exists across medications, the physician or patient may opt for an alternative other than one of the drugs originally prescribed. This may involve switching drugs within therapy classes to avoid any potential drug–drug interactions, or may involve removing one of the drugs from the therapeutic regimen and substituting a non-pharmaceutical treatment instead.

Comorbidity

Comorbidity is another correction that must be applied to calculating the potential market for a product. Comorbidity refers to a single patient with multiple disease states that may be treated by a single product. This is illustrated in Figure 3.10. In the illustration, the potential market size for the unipolar depression market is 200,000 patients and the potential size of the general anxiety disorder market is 100,000. The potential market size for a single product that treats both disorders is 270,000 (the total of the two independent indications minus the number of patients who are comorbid for both diseases).

Comorbidity is another correction that must be applied to calculating the potential market for a product.

Corrections for comorbidity can be done at two places in the forecast algorithm – either at the beginning of the algorithm (where comorbid patients are ascribed to only one of the two potential indications) or at the end of the forecast algorithm (where the product forecast is corrected downwards to remove the double counting of product revenues). Using the first approach is not recommended since it leads to an under-forecast of the therapy area from which the patients were removed. Using the second approach – removal of double-counted revenues from the product forecast – is recommended.

FORECASTING THE PRODUCT

Once the market potential has been modelled the forecaster is ready to proceed to the calculation of potential patients who are treated with the product being forecast. This is referred to as patient share, product share, or market share depending upon the definition of the share calculation. For purposes of discussion we will refer to this section using patient share. The elements of the algorithm presented in this section represent the 'product' section in Figure 3.2.

Defining the competitive mix

The first step in the calculation of patient share is to determine the appropriate product mix against which the forecast product will compete. This definition of the competitor list will govern much of the share construction algorithm in subsequent sections. As with the market definition, the definition of the competitor matrix is a judgement call of the forecaster and is another balancing act between simplicity and complexity.

The competitor matrix must include all products against which the product competes and may include both inter-class and intra-class competition. For example, a forecast for an oral anti-diabetic may include only other oral products or may include non-oral insulin products as well. A forecast for a hormonal receptor antagonist in breast cancer may include only other hormonal agents or may include classic chemotherapy as well. A forecast for a cyclooxygenase-2 (COX-2) inhibitor in rheumatoid arthritis may include only COX-2 inhibitors or may include non-steroidal anti-inflammatory drugs (NSAIDs) as well. The list of examples goes on and includes almost all therapy areas that one can forecast. It is easy to see the trade-offs that begin to emerge between a complex (that is, multi-class) and a simple (that is, single class) competitor matrix. Again, it is the job of the forecaster to determine this balance point. Referring back to the principles discussed in Chapter 1, the guidance is to create a forecast complex enough to appropriately model the market dynamics, but not so complex as to become an unwieldy (and implicitly inflexible) analytical tool.

It is important to note the interrelationship between the choice of the competitor matrix and the definition used for the percentage of patients treated with drug therapy used in constructing the market portion of the forecast. The assumptions used in both definitions must be aligned. For example, if the competitive mix for a product is defined as a biologic versus a small molecule therapy (for example, in rheumatoid arthritis) then the percentage of patients treated with drug therapy actually represents the percentage of patients treated with a biologic as opposed to the percentage of patients treated with a biologic or a small-molecule. The definition used in the competitive mix must match exactly with the definition used to define the drug-treated population.

It is also important to note that non-drug competitors – such as exercise and diet, lifestyle changes, alternative medicine, surgical interventions and watchful waiting – are not included in the competitor mix. The patients receiving these therapies have already been excluded from the competitive

The first step in the calculation of patient share is to determine the appropriate product mix against which the forecast product will compete.

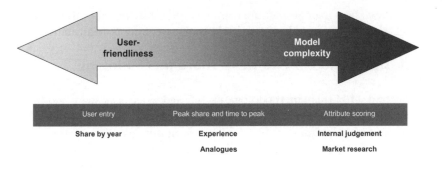

Selection of methodology depends on the:

- Objective of the forecast
- Data available
- Stage of development of the compound

Figure 3.11   Methods used in product share projection

Forecasting the
share of patients
who will receive
our product
versus the
competitors is
the heart of the
forecast model.

mix using the percentage drug-treated variable described in the market flow
section.

Forecasting patient share

Forecasting the share of patients who will receive our product versus the
competitor's is the heart of the forecast model. As with many choices in
forecasting, the modeller has the opportunity to balance simplicity against
complexity in choosing the method for share projection. Figure 3.11 presents
the methods used in share projection and their placement along a spectrum
of user-friendliness and model complexity.

User-entry share methodology

The simplest – and most user-friendly – method of share projection is user-
entry. In this methodology the forecaster enters the projected share for
all products in the competitive grid. Shares may be entered on a monthly,
quarterly, or annual basis, or entered on any time basis aligned with the
model design. The method is extremely simple – no complex calculation
routines are needed and the dynamics of product uptake (that is, how quickly
the product gains patients and therefore share in the market) is embedded
into the shares entered in by the user.

The difficulty with user-entry methodology is that the logic trail and thought
patterns used to construct the patient shares may not be readily transparent
or documented in the model. How the user reached the decisions regarding
patient share is not known. The thought process may have been extensive,
relying upon volumes of market research data that the user had assimilated.
Or the patient share call may have been based off a user prior experience with
similar products in similar markets. Or the forecaster may have entered in
numbers that were 'expected' by the organisation and therefore filled with

bias. Unless these logic strands are captured and documented in the forecast model the user-entry methodology lacks transparency and defensibility.

Peak share and time to peak share methodology

The second set of share methodologies is referred to as 'peak share and time to peak'. In this methodology the user enters in two parameters – the peak share of the product being forecast and the amount of time required to attain this forecast peak share. This method appears to be slightly more sophisticated than the simple user-entry method, because in this second case the user is decoupling the static (peak share) and dynamic (time to peak) assumptions in generating patient shares.

This methodology suffers from the same weakness in terms of transparency and defensibility as the simple user-share method. For the peak share estimate the same argument holds as discussed in the user-entry section. If the logic trail used by the user is not explicit or documented it becomes difficult – if not impossible – to judge the merits of the share assumption.

The lack of transparency around the time to peak assumption is even more dangerous. The assumptions used in determining the shape of the uptake of a new product (its adoption curve or penetration rate) have significant and direct consequences on the forecast itself. As we will see in the subsequent section on adoption curves, one of the biggest challenges to the forecaster is to predict the shape of this uptake curve. Many of the peak share and time to peak methodologies either pre-select the shape of the adoption curve, or only allow the user to select from a restricted family of adoption curves. This limitation in shaping the adoption curve in most time to peak methodologies significantly handicaps the veracity of this approach. Models that allow the user to overcome this limitation and allow the user to evaluate different – and transparent – shapes to the various adoption curves overcome the limitations and criticism described above.

Attribute methodologies

The third and most sophisticated method to forecast share for a product is based on the product's attributes, the market's perception of those attributes and the importance of the various attributes in the mind of the prescribing physician. There is a family of different methodologies that fall into this category – attribute scores and weights, conjoint studies, preference shares, discrete choice models, utility-function models and so forth. Each method is a different application in practice of similar theoretical underpinnings. Let's first examine the theory behind these methods and then their practical application.

The theory to the attribute methodology approach is shown in Figure 3.12. In this method of share projection, a product's usage is modelled as a function of its attributes and the importance of these attributes in the prescribing

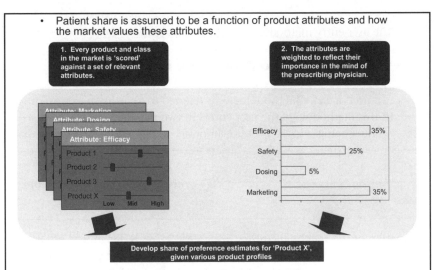

- Patient share is assumed to be a function of product attributes and how the market values these attributes.

1. Every product and class in the market is 'scored' against a set of relevant attributes.

2. The attributes are weighted to reflect their importance in the mind of the prescribing physician.

Attribute: Marketing
Attribute: Dosing
Attribute: Safety
Attribute: Efficacy

Product 1
Product 2
Product 3
Product X

Low   Mid   High

Efficacy — 35%
Safety — 25%
Dosing — 5%
Marketing — 35%

Develop share of preference estimates for 'Product X', given various product profiles

Figure 3.12   The attribute approach to share calculation

decision. The attributes used in the prescribing decision are very therapy-area-specific, but generally include some measure of efficacy and safety. Several markets also are sensitive to dosing schedule, form of product and so forth. In many markets, efficacy is divided into efficacy against the underlying disease state and efficacy against symptom expression. Safety may be divided into tolerability and nuisance side-effects versus other safety concerns, such as neutropenia and effects on liver function. The choice of which attributes to model in the forecast is determined by the therapy area being considered.

Once the attribute list is selected the forecaster must rank the products relative to each other on each attribute. This can be as simple as scoring the products relative to each other (for example, on a numerical scale) or as complex as a primary market research study where the respondents rank-order the products relative to each other.

When the rank-ordering of products is completed, the forecaster has a relative understanding of product perception within each attribute. Next, the attributes must be combined to reflect their importance in the prescribing decision. At a first approximation this is done by weighting each attribute to reflect its importance. For example, if efficacy is considered more important in the prescribing decision than safety it may be weighted at 75 per cent versus safety at 25 per cent. This weighting would reflect a threefold greater importance of efficacy than safety in the prescriber's mind.

A general example of this approach is shown in Table 3.2 in which three products are being scored in an attribute approach. The scale used in the efficacy scoring ranges from 1 to 10, with 10 being considered resolution of symptoms and 1 being no demonstration of efficacy. Similarly for safety, a score of 10 represents placebo-like side-effects and a score of 1 represents significant safety concerns leading to discontinuation of product use.

The choice of which attributes to model in the forecast is determined by the therapy area being considered.

Table 3.2 Calculation of shares based on scores and weights

Product	Efficacy score	Safety score	Efficacy weight	Safety weight	Weighted efficacy score	Weighted safety score	Combined score	Share (%)
A	10	4			7.5	1.0	8.5	45
B	6	2			4.5	0.5	5.0	26
C	4	10			3.0	2.5	5.5	29
Market			75%	25%			19.0	100

Calculation of the weighted efficacy and safety scores is dependent upon the relative weightings of each attribute in the market. For example, in Table 3.2 for Product A the weighted efficacy score is calculated as 10 multiplied by 75 per cent to result in 7.5. The weighted safety score is calculated as 4 multiplied by 25 per cent to yield a weighted safety score of 1.0. Similar calculations yield the weighted scores for Products B and C.

To calculate patient share the combined scores (see Table 3.2) are combined for each product and then divided by the total for the market. In Table 3.2 for Product A this is represented by the combined score of 8.5 divided by the market total score of 19.0 to result in a share of 45 per cent. Similar calculations for Products B and C yield shares for all products in the market.

Scores and weights

In the simplest application of the above theory the products are scored and the attributes weighted by a panel of experts – people who are knowledgeable in both the products and market dynamics. Within a company this can be done by members of the clinical team or by physicians serving on an advisory board. For a more broad-based view the forecaster can turn to focus groups of independent physicians or a quantitative market research study to obtain the scores and weights necessary in the share calculation exercise.

There are, however, practical considerations the forecaster must incorporate in the choice of how to gather the data.

Bias in the scoring

The first consideration is bias, which is encompassed in the two forms discussed in Chapter 1 – conscious and unconscious. In conscious bias the respondents who are scoring and weighting the products will over- or under-estimate the values to drive the results to a conclusion they already have formed in their minds. In this case the forecaster must facilitate the scoring exercise and probe at the underlying logic used to generate the scores and weights. Where the logic appears to be biased the forecaster must attempt to remove the bias – either through direct challenge of the scores or though verification of the scores and weights from other data sources.

Unconscious bias is more difficult to correct. In this case, the bias is due to the decision-makers acting upon an incomplete set of information. The evaluator may be aware of only a subset of the clinical trial data, or may be ascribing more weight to anecdotal data than warranted in generating the scores and weights, or may be reacting to a target product profile that is incomplete. In this case the forecaster must attempt to remove the bias by ensuring all the information is current and available to the people who are generating the scores and weights.

The choice of a scale

A second consideration in gathering product score data is the choice of the scale that is used in the scoring. The object of the scoring exercise is to place the products relative to each other on specific attributes. Although this relative ranking is the critical outcome, the respondents scoring the products need to be anchored in a scale. If the scale is not defined and anchored it is impossible to collect the responses from various respondents and blend the results into a single view of the market. The perception of one respondent who scores 8 on a 10-point scale must equal the perception of a second respondent who scores the product similarly. This anchoring is accomplished by defining the scale prior to product scoring. For example, on an efficacy variable this may equate to defining the high score as complete resolution of the disease, or as complete remission of the symptoms, or – in a case where complete resolution is not possible – a 20 per cent improvement in physiological function. The definition of a scale varies by therapy area, by attribute, and by the respondents' perceptions of the market. Any definition can be used – as long as it is consistently understood and agreed to by the respondents who are providing the scoring data.

The choice of interval

A third practical consideration in the product scoring approach is the interval selected on the scoring scale. In the discussion above the end points of the scale were discussed, but what about the interval in the scale? Does a twofold difference in score indicate a twofold difference in perception of the product attribute, or can this represent a minor improvement or a major change in perception instead? These are the questions that are addressed by the interval selected on the scoring scale. Figure 3.13 demonstrates some of the different scaling intervals that may be used in product scoring. The choice of the interval is critical to the scoring exercise as it translates the perceptions in the market into the difference rankings of the products. The challenge for the forecaster is to determine which of these interval scales – or another interval scale – is appropriate for the therapy area being forecast.

Unconscious bias is more difficult to correct.

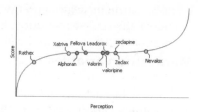

Difference in score is proportional to difference in perception.

Not an important attribute - difference in perception does not translate to difference in score.

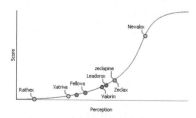

Not an important attribute unless the product stands out from the current standard of care – difference in perception translates to difference in score near the high end.

Not an important attribute unless the product is substantially inferior from the current standard of care – difference in perception translate to difference in score near the low end.

Figure 3.13   Examples of scales used in attribute scoring methods

The uncertainty of response

The fourth consideration around scoring is related to the uncertainty of response. As discussed in Chapter 1, there are inherent uncertainties in forecasting that need to be captured and transparent to the end-user of the forecast. Uncertainty in product perception (scores) falls into this modelling demand. The scores captured in this forecast methodology are used as surrogates in modelling the prescriber's behaviour. As such, these scores represent the prescriber perceptions of the products. If perception deviates from reality, the forecaster must ensure that the perceptions are captured in the forecast model. One method to capture the different perceptions that occur in product scoring is to capture a range of potential scores associated with each product. Once a range has been captured the scores can enter into the forecast algorithm using the simulation techniques discussed in Chapter 1.

Changes in perception over time

If perception deviates from reality, the forecaster must ensure that the perceptions are captured in the forecast model.

The next practical consideration involves changes in perception of the products over time – in essence, changing the scores over time as perception of the products change. Similar to other variables in the forecast model this can be accommodated by allowing the scores for a product to change over time, although it is important for the forecaster to distinguish between a product's attribute *scores* changing over time versus an attribute's *weight* changing. For example, if a product's perception of safety is changing over time, the score for that product associated with safety will change. If safety is becoming more – or less – important to the prescriber over time the weight of the safety attribute will change over time, but the scores associated with the individual product will not change.

Marketing variables

A sixth consideration in the attribute scoring approach involves the scores and weights assigned to marketing variables such as company reputation, sales force effort, marketing programmes, clinical publications and so forth. In prior discussions we have focused on clinical attributes such as efficacy and safety. There are, however, changes in prescribing behaviour that are due to commercial attributes, such as those described above. The forecaster must capture and model the effects of these commercial attributes on the prescribing decision. This presents a challenge because of the difficulty of measuring the effects of the commercial attributes. Direct measurement is not typically possible. When asked, the majority of physicians will discount the effects of marketing and sales efforts, giving low weights to the commercial variables in the prescribing decision. However, in many markets there are observable changes in prescribing behaviour when correlated to changes in marketing efforts and these changes must be modelled in the scores and weights. Frequently scores and weights for marketing attributes are determined through indirect analysis of behaviours in the therapy areas to be forecast.

When asked, the majority of physicians will discount the effects of marketing and sales efforts, giving low weights to the commercial variables in the prescribing decision.

Determination of weights

The final consideration in attribute methodologies relate to the determination of weights. To a first approximation the attribute weights apply to all products in the market. The logic of the construction is that the attributes apply to the prescribing decision, and products are measured against these attributes in the prescriber's mind when the product decision is taken. Under this logic the weights used to model the market apply to each of the products in the market equally. Changes in market dynamics – such as an increased emphasis on safety – are modelled by increasing the importance of this attribute over time. A more refined method of modelling would be to allow for product-specific weights as opposed to exclusively market weights. In this refinement, the prescribing decision is assumed to value each product independently with respect to the attribute combinations. For example, under this construct a product that has a poor safety profile and is being considered in a safety-sensitive market would have more emphasis placed on safety than a product that has a good safety profile. The prescribing decision for the safety-poor product will be more heavily weighted towards safety than the prescribing decision for the safer product. The poor safety profile for the example product trumps the prescribing decision in a safety sensitive therapy area. Analogous statements could be made for the other attributes. Although this refinement of product-specific weights is analytically correct the challenges to model construction often preclude its use in routine forecast models.

A summary of the various share estimation techniques and their pros and cons is shown in Table 3.3.

Product
adoption
is called
many things
– adoption
curves, uptake
models, product
diffusion,
dissemination
curves and so
forth.

Table 3.3   Evaluation of different share projection methodologies

Methodology	Pros	Cons
User-entry	• Flexible and quick • Simple model construction	• Logic used to derive shares can be unclear • Defensibility relies upon user documentation • Combines peak share and uptake dynamics in a single forecast input
Peak share and time to peak	• Separates peak share from the dynamics of uptake • Simple model construction	• Logic used to derive shares can be unclear • Defensibility relies upon user documentation • Shape of the uptake curve is critical and often inflexible
Attribute scores and weights	• Constructs share as a function of product attributes • Separates attributes used in the prescribing decision • Allows for perceptual mapping of products • Forecasts are defensible based upon product attributes	• Outcome relies upon the integrity of the input data; bias can affect results • Data collection can be costly and time-consuming

Product adoption

In user-entry share methods the dynamics of peak share and uptake are collapsed into a single assumption. In the other methodologies these two dynamics – peak share and time to peak – are modelled separately. This section examines the theory and application of product adoption. As with share projection methods, we will first present the theory behind product adoption and then examine the practical application of theory.

Product adoption is called many things – adoption curves, uptake models, product diffusion, dissemination curves and so forth. All represent the time required for a product to be tested and used in the marketplace. As an increasing number of individuals use the product its penetration of the market grows. This growth continues until the product has been tried by all

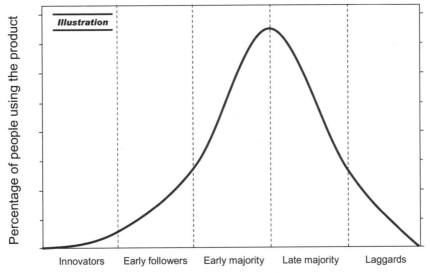

Figure 3.14 The distribution of users of new products

the potential users. At this point the product is referred to as 100 per cent adopted in the market.

Although always present in market dynamics, adoption curve theory was examined in the literature in the early 1960s. A seminal book on product diffusion was published by Rogers in 1962.[1] In this text Rogers describes a distribution associated with potential users of any new product, as shown in Figure 3.14. In this example a small set of individuals use the product when it first appears on the market – the innovators. These first users are followed by the 'early followers' and then the 'early majority'. Relatively late in the adoption sequence the 'late majority' uses the product, followed finally by the 'laggards'. Once all the laggards have tried the product there are no more potential users left and the product would be fully adopted in the marketplace and would have obtained its peak share of users.

Using this example we can translate the number of users of the product to the revenue generated by those users. This is illustrated in Figure 3.15. It is this translation of new users over time into revenue that gives rise to the S-shaped adoption curve seen in Figure 3.15. This curve also is called a Bass Diffusion Model, a Gompertz Curve, or a Type 1 Curve. The revenue curve can be described by a mathematical equation as shown in Figure 3.16.

What if we were able to compress the amount of time required for adoption?

What if we were able to compress the amount of time required for adoption? If users adopt the product faster – that is, the amount of time required for product use and adoption is decreased – the adoption curve shifts to the one shown in Figure 3.17. This adoption curve is referred to as fast uptake or a Type 2 curve. Conversely if the amount of time required for adoption

1 Rogers, E. M. (1962) *Diffusion of Innovations*, New York: The Free Press.

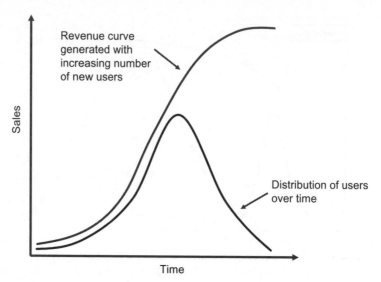

Figure 3.15   Conversion of users into product revenue

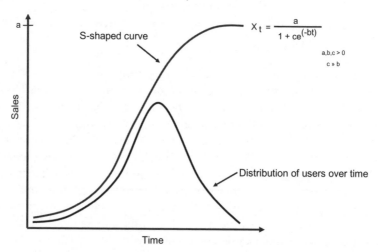

Figure 3.16   Mathematical representation of an S-shaped adoption curve

The slow uptake curve, on the other hand, has a different mathematical form in the early years of adoption.

of the product is lengthened, the product adopts more slowly in the market, generating the adoption curve shown in Figure 3.18. This is referred to as a slow uptake curve.

It is important to note the differences in the mathematical equations used to describe these three types of adoption curves. The S-shaped (Type 1) and fast uptake (Type 2) curves have the same mathematical form – only the values of the constants in the equation vary (see Figures 3.16 and 3.17). The slow uptake curve, on the other hand, has a different mathematical form in the early years of adoption. When modelling adoption curves many programs allow only the inclusion of Type 1 or Type 2 curves because the software relies upon a single mathematical expression. In the section describing peak share and time to peak methodologies we mentioned the dangers associated with time to peak methodologies that do not allow flexibility of the adoption

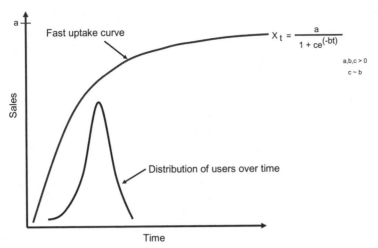

Figure 3.17 Compression of adoption time leads to a fast uptake curve

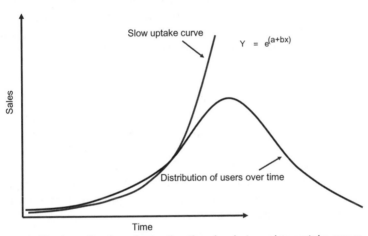

Figure 3.18 Lengthening of adoption time leads to a slow uptake curve

curve. In essence, the lack of flexibility can be due to the limitation of forecast software programs to allow only Type 1 or Type 2 curves. This is a limitation the forecaster needs to be aware of and to probe in selecting time to peak algorithms.

The desired adoption curve for most pharmaceutical products is the fast uptake curve. Many marketing and sales strategies are directed towards accelerating product adoption such that the fast uptake curve is realised. Classically this is done by segmenting a group of potential prescribers into the behaviours aligned with adoption – that is, rapid adopters, the early majority, the late majority and laggards. Targeting marketing and sales messages to the appropriate group at the appropriate time increases the efficiency of the marketing and sales message and results in more rapid adoption. For example, targeting early adopters in the launch phase of a product's lifecycle is more productive than targeting laggards. Analogously, marketing effort directed towards early adopters when the product is late in its lifecycle is wasted effort since the prescribers already are using the product. This concept of physician

Many marketing and sales strategies are directed towards accelerating product adoption such that the fast uptake curve is realised.

NEW PRODUCT
FORECASTING

segmentation and targeting to increase the efficiency of the marketing and sales message rapidly has become the norm in the pharmaceutical industry.

Regulatory approval date

The start of the adoption process for a product is linked to its regulatory approval date, its launch date, product appearance in the market, the ability of prescribers to write a prescription for the product and the ability of the patient to get the prescription filled. These factors are rarely aligned such that a single date governs the start of the adoption curve. Once a product receives regulatory approval there is a period of time required to stock distributors and educate the market that the product is available. Once available in the distribution channel, prescribers need the ability to write a prescription for the product. Frequently this is linked to an approval process on formularies or national reimbursement lists. In many countries the manufacturer needs to negotiate price with the various pricing authorities before physicians can prescribe the product. All of these activities have time elements associated with them that affect the preliminary uptake of the product. The forecaster must incorporate all these dynamics into the shape of the adoption when forecasting the product.

Adoption curves also must be aligned with the segmentation pattern used in modelling the market. If the segmentation was preserved through the share generation exercise it also must be preserved in generating adoption curves by the relevant segments. In some cases segmentation may be introduced at this stage in the algorithm if there are differential uptake dynamics in various segments. For example, in a forecast for the Canadian market the adoption curves need to be generated by province to account for differential formulary acceptance rates at the provincial level.

Adoption curve theory

The theory behind adoption curves is well developed and has been demonstrated for a number of non-pharmaceutical products, such as cell phones, steam irons, hybrid corn and so forth. Unfortunately for the pharmaceutical forecaster there are few products that conform to theory in the pharmaceutical markets. The reasons for this are multifold – the dynamics of pharmaceutical prescribing are complex, where the initial decision-maker (the physician), the intermediate decision-maker (typically the payer), and the final decision-maker (the patient) all can influence the final consumption of the product. Pharmaceutical products also are sensitive to competition in the markets. The adoption curve of a product marketed in isolation from competition is not the same as a product facing competitors in the marketplace. Third, aspects of product performance may be discovered only once the product is in the market. For example, safety issues discovered after a product is launched into the marketplace can significantly dampen, or even reverse, a product's upward adoption pattern.

Finally, pharmaceutical products are sensitive to promotion and the application of various market and sales programmes can affect a product's uptake pattern. As discussed earlier, programmes such as segmentation and targeting of the prescribers will affect product uptake. Forecasting the magnitude of the effect, however, is a difficult exercise. Because of the complexity of the market setting up control groups to gauge the effects of promotion is extremely difficult. These difficulties compound to make generating adoption curves *ab initio* a very difficult exercise for the forecaster.

Analogue analysis and selection

The predominant approach in generating adoption curves is that of analogue analysis. In this approach the forecaster searches for product analogues that have launched to the market prior to the product being forecast. Once an appropriate analogue is identified the forecaster can then examine the historical uptake pattern for the analogue and apply this uptake pattern to the new product being forecast.

In selecting an appropriate analogue the forecaster must compare across a number of dimensions, as shown in Figure 3.19. Rarely – if ever – will the forecaster find a 'perfect' analogue that replicates all the dynamics of the market. Rather, the forecaster finds a market basket of potential analogues, all of which have some degree of commonality with the product to be forecast. In these situations the forecaster needs to understand the 'stories' told by each analogue product and to determine the extent to which the analogue's performance can be used as a surrogate for the product of forecast interest.

This difficulty of selecting an appropriate analogue for a product's adoption coupled with the importance of the adoption pattern to the forecast,

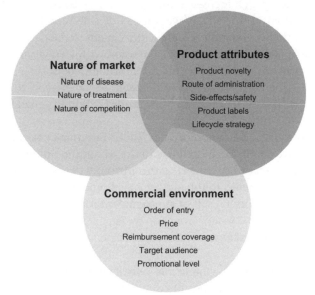

The predominant approach in generating adoption curves is that of analogue analysis.

Figure 3.19   Criteria used in selecting product analogues

especially in the early years, makes this variable one of the most significant in the forecast. In fact, erroneous assumptions around this variable is most often responsible for wrong forecasts. As discussed in Chapter 2, variables that have a significant effect on the results and for which there are strong elements of uncertainty, the preferred modelling system is to create a series of scenario forecasts. In evaluating the effects of adoption, the forecaster should create a series of product forecasts using different adoption curves. This allows both the forecaster and the end-user of the forecast to gauge the effects of adoption on the product forecast and to represent transparently the uncertainty introduced due to imperfect analogues.

Cannibalisation

The final dynamic to model in the share projection section of the new product forecast algorithm is that of cannibalisation. Cannibalisation refers to the conversion of patients between two formulations of a product – typically a strategy used for line extensions of a currently marketed product. When conversion occurs the second product is said to cannibalise the first.

For the forecaster, cannibalisation can be divided into two dynamics: passive and active.

Cannibalisation can offer several benefits. From a therapeutic perspective introduction of a new formulation may enhance the therapeutic benefit of a product – for example, by introducing longer steady-state levels of the therapeutic ingredient in the patient. A new formulation may enhance compliance – such as once-daily dosing being introduced to replace a product that currently is dosed at three times per day. Many line extension introductions are designed to address this need.

A manufacturer also can introduce line extensions as part of their lifecycle strategy for a product. In this case the line extension may offer a benefit to the manufacturer through increased pricing or prolonged patent protection or marketing exclusivity. If the advantage from a line extension is solely to the manufacturer – that is, there is no therapeutic benefit to the patient – there is a risk that the market will view the line extension with scepticism and that a public policy issue may arise. If the line extension does offer both therapeutic benefits to the patient as well as financial benefit to the manufacturer, the dynamics of the forecast follow those for cannibalisation in general.

For the forecaster, cannibalisation can be divided into two dynamics: passive and active. Passive cannibalisation refers to the reallocation of market share based solely on the market's reaction to the attributes of the line extension. Active cannibalisation refers to the movement of product share from the old to the new formulation as a result of a company's promotional efforts.

Passive cannibalisation

Passive cannibalisation can be forecast is several ways. If the base forecast is constructed using the attribute score and weights methodology the new shares can be forecast as a function of the difference in score for the new formulation in the selected attributes that have changed. The new score for the line extension will translate into market share depending upon the market's weighting of the attribute that has changed. For example, in a market that values dosing schedules, the movement from a twice-daily to a once-daily formulation will gain market share (assuming the once daily is the preferred dosing form) depending upon the significance of the perceptual separation of the two dosing forms (the score) and the importance of the attribute (the weight).

A second way to forecast passive cannibalisation is through the use of product analogues. Examining historical data for line extension introduction of other products provides a basis for the forecast. For example, the introduction of extended-release formulations in the cardiovascular markets has extensive prior history and use of product analogues will help to forecast the introduction of a new extended formulation product in these markets.

Active cannibalisation

Active cannibalisation is more difficult to forecast. The degree of movement between shares typically is a result of the marketing efforts of the manufacturer who is directing the switch. It is the result of the marketing resources coupled with the effectiveness of the marketing message that results in the degree of active cannibalisation. The most extreme form of active cannibalisation is for a manufacturer to withdraw the current formulation from the market once the line extension has been launched. This effectively forces the market to switch from the old to the new formulation. As mentioned above, if the reason for the new product introduction to the marketplace is purely financial and this is apparent to the market, withdrawal of the current formulation can have significant public policy implications.

It is the result of the marketing resources coupled with the effectiveness of the marketing message that results in the degree of active cannibalisation.

CONVERTING PATIENTS TO REVENUE

Once the number of patients on product has been determined the forecaster must convert these patients to volume, prescription, revenue and net income forecasts (Figure 3.2). These conversion factors begin by converting patients to volume through a series of assumptions related to dosing, compliance and persistence (Figure 3.20).

If there are multiple dosing forms for the product the forecaster must apply the product mix assumptions at this point. For example, if there are two formulations in the market – a 50 mg and a 100 mg formulation – the forecaster must determine the number of patients on each formulation before proceeding with the compliance, persistence and pricing assumptions. In cases where products are titrated (that is, patients move through a series of dosing strengths until they reach a strength where the therapy is optimised) the forecaster must apply the titration assumptions – length of time on a

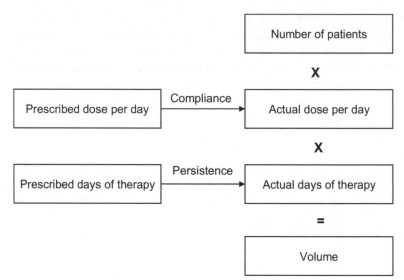

Figure 3.20   Converting patients to volume

given therapy before up- or down-titration occurs, and the final equilibrium mix of patients in each dosing strength.

The multiplication of patients on each dosing strength by the theoretical number of doses per treatment period (year, month, week and so forth) yields the theoretical volume, assuming patients are 100 per cent compliant and persistent. The effects of compliance and persistence are to lower this theoretical upper boundary to an actual level of product consumed in the specified time period.

Forecasting compliance and persistence

The dynamics represented by compliance and persistence are different. Compliance refers to a patient's behaviour in taking the prescribed dose per day. Persistence refers to a patient continuing on therapy and receiving refills in a timely manner. These differences are illustrated in Figure 3.21. In reality the two variables combine to yield the actual days of therapy in a given year, and frequently forecasters will combine them into a single variable, usually called compliance. The reason for the initial splitting of the variable into two parts was to acknowledge the difference in market dynamics, and to suggest that marketing programmes can better affect persistence than they can affect compliance. Therefore, programmes aimed at increasing patient persistence on a given therapy would result in an increase in revenue.

Finding data for compliance and persistence assumptions can be a challenge for the forecaster. Few secondary data sources are available to offer compliance and persistence rates. It is possible to use analogue data, using prescription or days of therapy data from the audits (both of these measures already include the effects of compliance and persistence since they record actual pills dispensed), but the source of patient counts (the denominator in the back-

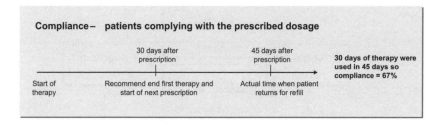

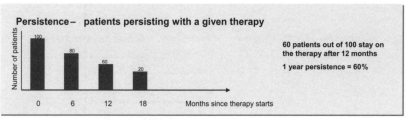

Figure 3.21 Compliance and persistence

Although this is a simple calculation the effects of the pricing assumption are dramatic.

calculation of compliance and persistence) frequently is difficult to obtain. Using data from clinical trials affords an overestimate of compliance and persistence rates due to the monitoring involved in clinical trials. With the recent advent of patient-level data (longitudinal patient studies) the forecaster will have a better source of compliance and persistence data in the future.

After correcting for compliance and persistence the forecaster has a volume forecast. This represents the volume of product required assuming the compliance and persistence rates specified in the forecast. In terms of a volume forecast this typically represents the lowest required amount to be produced. Corrections for potentially higher compliance and persistence rates, safety stock in manufacturing and distributors' inventory holdings still need to be applied. At this point assumptions of the length of prescription may be applied to obtain a forecast for total prescriptions dispensed in the market. Assumptions about new patient starts and refill rates may be applied to yield a forecast for new prescriptions dispensed. Although neither of these calculations is required for the forecast of revenue, both prescription volume numbers are used to monitor the performance of a product once it launches to the market and is tracked by the various pharmaceutical audit vendors.

The final step in the conversion of patients to revenue is to convert the volume calculations into revenue. This is done by applying the pricing assumption to the underlying volume measure (price per tablet, price per cycle of therapy, price per injection and so forth). Although this is a simple calculation the effects of the pricing assumption are dramatic. Once a price has been identified the forecaster needs to revisit every assumption in the forecast model and ensure that the assumption is aligned with the assumed price. This is because price, and its effects on reimbursement and market demand, affects many of the forecast variables (Figure 3.22).

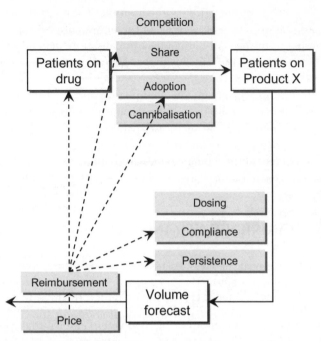

Figure 3.22 The ubiquitous effects of price and reimbursement

The effects of price on the percentage of patients who receive drug treatment may arise from patient sensitivity to cost (if the patient is paying directly) or from payer sensitivity to cost (where certain drug classes may not be reimbursed, limiting patient access). Frequently tiering of drug therapy is used – where patients and physicians must move through a predetermined order of drug classes in selecting a therapy. If the physician is sensitive to price, their prescribing decision may be altered depending upon the price comparisons between competing products. In this case, price would be an attribute that would be included in modelling the prescribing decision.

One of the most visible effects of the price assumption is on the adoption curve. Depending upon the assumed price and the length of reimbursement negotiations, the actual launch of a product in the market may be delayed. For example, if a product is priced at a level that requires substantial time for reimbursement negotiations the time between product approval and actual usage in the market may be significant. Pricing negotiations, and reimbursement decisions, can take place at a national level, at a state or provincial level, at a health-care plan level, or at an individual hospital level. When such divisions occur in the pricing negotiations the forecaster must estimate the percentage of the market affected by the negotiating entities and correct for the differential launch dates. This is frequently seen in Canadian markets where negotiations take place at the provincial level and in the United States markets, where negotiations take place with insurers who cover a large number of potential patients.

One of the most visible effects of the price assumption is on the adoption curve.

Price also can affect the degree of cannibalisation of a new formulation on an existing formulation. The relative price of the newer entity compared to the existing product can speed up or retard cannibalisation, depending upon the relative price difference and the sensitivity of the market to price.

Another effect of price can be to alter compliance and persistence rates. For patients who have a high degree of polypharmacy the aggregate cost of medications can be large. In such cases patients may elect to alter their dosing, or split their doses, in an effort to control drug costs. This has been observed in markets in the United States with patients who experience a high pill burden (and therefore perhaps a cost burden) due to polypharmacy.

FINAL CONSIDERATIONS

This chapter considered the tools, methods, and algorithms appropriate for forecasting products before they are launched in the market. Once the product is launched in the market the forecaster has the luxury of data and history, which leads to a change in methodology and approaches to forecasting. We will discuss these history-rich methods in the next chapter.

CHAPTER 4

In-Market Product Forecasting

The most essential qualification for a politician is the ability to foretell what will happen tomorrow, next month, and next year, and to explain afterwards why it did not happen.

Winston Churchill

No data yet. It is a capital mistake to theorise before you have all of the evidence.

Sherlock Holmes

With the advent of a product's introduction into the market a new consideration comes into play – the generation of time series data.

The previous chapter explored forecasting methods that are applicable prior to a product's launch into the market. With the advent of a product's introduction into the market a new consideration comes into play – the generation of time series data. This chapter will present techniques related to in-market (also called current product) forecasting. As discussed in Chapter 2, the methods available to the forecaster now include statistical time series tools in addition to the judgement-rich methods discussed in prior chapters (see Figure 2.7).

Does this mean that the forecaster can use purely statistical techniques to evaluate historical data and project future trends? If so, shouldn't the forecasts become more 'accurate' as the uncertainty inherent in judgemental data disappears? The answer to both questions is absolutely not. We will explore the justification for this answer in this chapter, presenting best practices for in-market forecasting.

IN-MARKET PRODUCT FORECAST ALGORITHM

The general algorithm used for in-market forecasting is shown in Figure 4.1. It can be modified for specific therapy areas and products, but the general

Baseline trends

Market baseline trend
(Time series data)

Product baseline trend
(Time series data)

Environmental change	Marketing strategy
Policy change	Sales strategy
Competitor activity	Other ex-trend events

Ex-trend events

Market projection
(Trend and ex-trend events)

Product demand projection
(Trend and ex-trend events)

Channel corrections

Distributor activity

Parallel imports

Reconciliation

and conversion

Product ex-factory forecast

Figure 4.1   Generalised in-market product forecast algorithm

The subtleties of trending, however, are much more complex, and selecting the appropriate approach for trending historical data is the first key judgement a forecaster makes for in-market forecasting.

sections of the algorithm remain invariant: trend historical data; apply the effects of ex-trend events; and convert the trended data into the required forecast outputs.

TREND HISTORICAL DATA

The first step in the algorithm is to use historical data to examine market and product performance. Trending the historical data often is viewed as a purely statistical exercise, where a software program accepts the historical data inputs and returns a 'best fit' trend line that projects performance into the future. In the simplest case, this trending occurs when an individual simply places a ruler against a graph of historical data points and draws a projected line into the future. The subtleties of trending, however, are much more complex, and selecting the appropriate approach for trending historical data is the first key judgement a forecaster makes for in-market forecasting.

Trending algorithms

In Chapter 2 various methods for trending time series data were presented in Figure 2.7. A definition of each of these statistical techniques is given in the Appendix. There are a number of software programs available to the forecaster; each software package performs these varied trending algorithms almost effortlessly. Every valid approach seeks to fit the time series data to a trend line that minimises the deviation between the actual data and the predicted data from the trending algorithm (usually referred to as minimisation of the root mean square error of the trend). Differences in software packages arise primarily from the user interfaces (both for input and output of the data) and the number of potential methods used to fit the historical data points. Almost all trending software programs will handle complexities such as seasonality.

Many excellent software reviews have been conducted on trending algorithms.[1] Rather than repeat these reviews here we will focus on two key challenges to the forecaster in performing trend analysis: selecting the underlying datasets to trend and selecting the appropriate number of historical datapoints for the analysis.

Selecting the underlying datasets to trend

The pharmaceutical industry is both blessed and cursed by data. There are a number of data sources and inputs available for time series analysis: total prescriptions, new prescriptions, total units, units by stock keeping unit, units by strength, days of therapy, patient days, retail units, hospital units, Internet pharmacy units, sales to wholesalers, wholesaler and retail pharmacy inventories and so forth. The blessing is that each of these datasets gives the forecaster insights into market dynamics, which can vary slightly between the datasets because of the different dynamic each measures. The curse is that comparison of trends across datasets may yield dramatically different results. These results may not be due to errors in the underlying data or in the trending algorithm, but may simply be due to the interconversion factor between datasets.

For example, consider the data shown in Figure 4.2. This graph presents the historical data for two different datasets for a single product – total prescriptions (TRx) and patients. Cursory examination of the total prescription trend line suggests that the product has not been growing over time, and a projection of this trend results in a flat or decelerating forecast for the product (assuming the TRx to revenue conversion was constant). Focusing on the patient data suggests that the product is growing as the number of patients increases, again assuming that the patient to revenue conversion was constant. Trending the patient data would result in an accelerating forecast.

The pharmaceutical industry is both blessed and cursed by data.

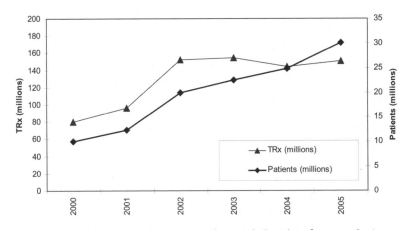

Figure 4.2   Historical patient and total prescription data for a product

1   Makridakis, S., Wheelwright, S. C. and Hyndman, R. J. (1998) *Forecasting Methods and Applications*, 3rd edn, New York: John Wiley & Sons, Inc.

Which interpretation of the data is correct? Without knowing the interconversion between patients and total prescriptions we cannot answer that question. If the explanation is that the length of the prescription dispensed for a given patient is increasing, then presumably the revenue also is increasing as the value of the prescription increases. This results in a growing revenue forecast. Conversely, if the number of prescriptions dispensed per patient is decreasing (perhaps due to a faster perceived resolution of disease) the value per patient is decreasing and the revenue forecast would be flat or decelerating. The key to forecasting the product is to understand the underlying market dynamics, as evidenced by the illustrative data presented in this example.

Often a naive forecaster, or a naive reviewer of a forecast, will focus exclusively on one dataset. This myopic and dangerous act will often result in erroneous forecasts. However, the other balance point in trending historical data – that of analysing every conceivable dataset – also can result in a confusion of results. For example, many organisations review weekly prescription data and attempt to forecast these data as an indicator of future product performance. This can be a valuable exercise if the data integrity is strong and the prescription data is representative of the market dynamics (that is, there are no interconversion issues related to prescription length or size). However, trending weekly data also can be a very time-consuming exercise for the forecaster and, if the data integrity is weak, can result in erroneous conclusions.

Where then is the balance point for trending historical data? The overarching principle is to use the historical measures that can be most accurately tracked and that best represent historical market dynamics. Significant errors in data reporting will translate into significant errors in trending and forecasting. The integrity of the underlying dataset is paramount. Assuming valid data, at a minimum the forecaster should examine the datasets presented in Table 4.1. These data capture slightly different dynamics in the market that allow the forecaster to triangulate historical activity.

The overarching principle is to use the historical measures that can be most accurately tracked and that best represent historical market dynamics.

Ultimately the forecaster should trend as many datasets as are available and relevant to the particular therapy area under analysis. This should be done for both the product in question as well as the market in total. Similar to the insights gained from trending multiple datasets relevant to the product, trending market data relative to product data leads to insights on product performance as well as overall market growth (or decline).

Two common data elements that have been conspicuously absent from this discussion are market share and product revenue. Both of these datasets are derivatives – that is, market share results from the division of product volume by market volume (where volume may be measured by prescriptions, units, days of therapy, or patients), and product revenue results from the multiplication of product volume by price. Trending either of these two derivative datasets can be misleading and result in erroneous conclusions.

Table 4.1   Data useful in trending historical market dynamics

Dataset	Comments
Total prescriptions (TRx)	Measures the ongoing activity of the prescribing physician – the demand generated in treating patients. Best unit of measure of underlying demand in a market where competing therapies have different lengths of therapy. A readily available measure for most retail pharmaceuticals, but may not be available or applicable for hospital-based or non-retail products.
New prescriptions (NRx)	Measures the initial prescribing behaviour of the physician. Useful as an indicator of product growth in the initial launch phase of a product but not directly translatable into total product demand or as a measure of market potential.
Units	Measures the number of units dispensed. The most direct measurement of demand and the most direct translation of prescribing activity into revenue. Usually the best unit of measure for non-retail based products. Audits of unit data dispensed may not be available in the retail sector. Difficult to calculate market share of prescriptions of patients since this requires knowing the average number of units per prescription or per patient.
Days of therapy (DOT)	Measures the days of therapy dispensed for a product. A measurement of patient usage of dispensed products. Useful for measuring market dynamics when products of differing therapy duration are dispensed in a market. Audits of days of therapy data may not be available in all markets, and calculation of prescription and patient market shares are difficult due to conversion factors similar to the above.
Patients	Measures the patients using pharmaceutical products in a given therapy area. A useful measure for comparing actual versus potential use based on the maximum number of patients. Typically patient audits are difficult to obtain except in specialised areas such as oncology or HIV disease. Patient data must be correctly translated into prescription or unit data before a revenue forecast can be obtained in order to correct for compliance and persistence.

These two different dynamics in the market are indistinguishable if only market share is trended.

For example, if one trends a growth in market share it is impossible to know *a priori* if this is a result of an increase in product volume (the numerator) or a decrease in market volume (the denominator). These two different dynamics in the market are indistinguishable if only market share is trended.

IN-MARKET
PRODUCT
FORECASTING

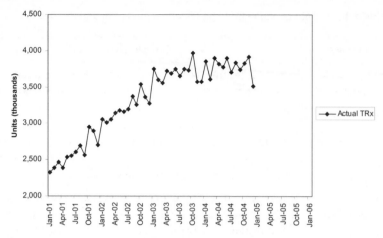

Once the appropriate identity of the datasets to trend has been determined the forecaster then is faced with the question of how many historical data points to include in the trend analysis.

Figure 4.3   An example of historical product performance

Analogously, trending revenue changes without knowing the change in true price (that is, list price corrected for product mix, discounts and rebates) clouds the true change in market dynamics. Trending of revenue also involves other issues that will be discussed in the reconciliation and conversion section of this chapter.

As we can see, what seemingly was a straightforward data trending exercise for time series data also involves a judgemental component – what is (or are) the best representative historical dataset(s) upon which to form the baseline trend analysis? In the next section we will encounter another judgement call the forecaster must make in performing the statistical trend analyses.

Select the time period for trending

Once the appropriate identity of the datasets to trend has been determined the forecaster then is faced with the question of how many historical data points to include in the trend analysis. Consider the data shown in Figure 4.3, which illustrates performance for a product. The forecaster must select the number of datapoints to include in the historical trend analysis.

After steady growth from 2001 through 2003, there appears to be a flattening of product performance in 2004. What is the appropriate number of historical datapoints to use in the time series trending? Figure 4.4 shows the results of three simple options: trending from January 2001 through December 2004, from January 2002 through December 2004, and from January 2003 through December 2004 (48, 36, and 24 months of historical data respectively). Inspection of this graph indicates very different projections for 2005 depending upon the number of historical datapoints chosen for the trend analysis. Simple trending algorithms were used for this example, and more complex algorithms may decrease the differences between the trend lines. However, the dilemma of the number of datapoints to trend remains the

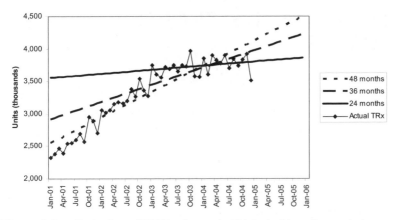

Figure 4.4   Projection of 2005 using varied historical trending periods

same: should the forecaster select a complete dataset or a dataset that is most 'representative' of current market conditions?

Which set of time series data should the forecaster use in projecting demand in 2005? The answer depends upon the reason for the flattening of the historical data in 2004. If the data truly represent a flattening of market demand due to changes in the environment, physician demand, or other factors that represent 'true' market dynamics the forecaster should use these data since they are the most representative of the future environment. On the other hand, if demand in 2004 was decreased due to constraints such as supply issues or a temporary reduction in marketing resources, the full dataset may be used for the forward projection. Once again, this is a judgement call that the forecaster must make in selecting the number of historical datapoints.

Statistics and trending software packages can lend insight to this decision... but they may be misleading as well. A naive view of statistics would tell the forecaster to select the number of historical datapoints that yields the best fit of historical data to the statistical trend analysis (that is, the trend that minimises root mean square error). In the simplified example above this would be the regression based on 48 months of data. As discussed, this may be the wrong decision if the market events captured in the latest 12 months of data truly represent the environment moving forward – in which case the forecaster must override the statistical best fit and select only 12 months of historical data for the trend analysis. Other statistical techniques – such as moving annual totals or dampening of recent datapoints – may be used to enhance the statistical outcomes and provide a better 'best fit' trend line, but none of these techniques can alleviate the necessity of the forecaster making a judgement call on the validity of the historical data. For reviews of in-market forecasts, the first question that should be asked of the forecaster is: 'How many datapoints were selected for the time series analysis and why?'

Once the optimal trend analysis has been established for both the product and the market, the forecaster next turns to quantifying the effect of ex-trend events on these baseline projections.

For reviews of in-market forecasts, the first question that should be asked of the forecaster is: 'How many datapoints were selected for the time series analysis and why?'

IN-MARKET
PRODUCT
FORECASTING

APPLYING THE EFFECTS OF EX-TREND EVENTS

What are ex-trend events? Simply stated, they are any activities that occur which are not reflected in the historical data. This all-encompassing definition includes events such as government policy revisions, changes in reimbursement environments, evolution in medical treatment paradigms, changes in marketing programmes, reallocation of sales resources, adverse publicity, new competition in the market and so forth. There are a number of ex-trend events that can occur and affect the baseline trend projections discussed in the previous section. The challenge to the forecaster is to identify these events and quantify the effects of the events on the forecast.

Ex-trend events fall into two broad categories – external changes outside direct control of the company and internal changes governed by the company itself. The external changes are the result of policy set by external agents – governments, insurers, physicians, public policy organisations, competitors and so forth. Internal ex-trend events are under the control of the company and typically involve changes in marketing and sales strategies for given products and the launch of line-extension products.

The challenge to the forecaster is to identify these events and quantify the effects of the events on the forecast.

External ex-trend events

External ex-trend events include examples such as changes in the regulatory review process in the European Union, the advent of physician drug budgets in Germany, the expansion of Medicare Part D coverage in the US and the rise of Internet pharmacy dispensing in Canada. Other examples include publicity in the public domain – such as controversy over suicide associated with certain classes of anti-depressants, safety issues associated with certain weight loss products, product withdrawals due to safety concerns and so forth. Still more examples arise from the launch of new competing products (or therapies) in the market, the loss of marketing exclusivity for currently marketed products, or patient access to specific health care plans and providers.

Although these examples are very diverse, the general approach for evaluating the effects of these events is to estimate three parameters:

1. the magnitude of the effect;
2. the timing of the effect; and
3. the products affected by the event.

Each of these parameters may be measured using the judgemental techniques discussed in Chapter 2, such as primary and secondary market research data and analogue analysis. For some ex-trend events we may need to use scenario analysis to model several alternative outcomes – for example, quantifying the effects of potential pricing changes.

Table 4.2   Share theft matrices

Ex-trend event: Launch of a new product
Magnitude of the event: New product gains 20% share of market

Magnitude of the ex-trend event assuming equal effects on all products

	Current share (%)	Share theft (source of new product share) (%)	Adjusted share (%)	Adjusted share calculation (%)
Product 1	10	25	5	5 = 10 - (25)(20)
Product 2	20	25	15	15 = 20 - (25)(20)
Product 3	30	25	25	25 = 30 - (25)(20)
Product 4	40	25	35	35 = 40 - (25)(20)
New product	0		20	20
TOTAL	100	100	100	

Magnitude of the ex-trend event assuming disproportionate effects on all products

	Current share (%)	Share theft (source of new product share) (%)	Adjusted share (%)	Adjusted share calculation (%)
Product 1	10	10	8	8 = 10 - (15)(20)
Product 2	20	15	17	17 = 20 - (15)(20)
Product 3	30	25	25	25 = 30 - (25)(20)
Product 4	40	50	30	30 = 40 - (50)(20)
New product	0		20	20
TOTAL	100	100	100	

Estimating the magnitude of the effect is akin to peak share analysis – what is the change in forecast product share due to the ex-trend event? The timing of the effect measures the dynamics of the ex-trend event – how quickly will the peak share effect be realised and, if applicable, how quickly will its effects diminish. The last parameter – the products affected by the ex-trend event – enables the forecaster to model disproportionate effects in the market. For example, changes in reimbursement status for a particular class of products may affect all products equally in that class (if they are priced similarly) or may affect some products more than others (presumably the higher-priced products in this example might be more affected than lower-priced products in the same class). This last parameter sometimes is referred to as the 'share theft matrix'. Essentially the effects of magnitude and timing of an ex-trend event are projected differentially for each affected product, rather than for each product equally. This is illustrated in Table 4.2.

Introduction of new competitors

Table 4.2 also illustrates another significant external ex-trend event the forecaster often encounters – the launch of a new competitor to the market. It demonstrates the method for estimating the effects of the new competitor on in-market product shares, but how does the forecaster measure the magnitude of the new competitor market share (for example, the 20 per cent share assumed for the new product in Table 4.2). This is accomplished using the new product forecasting techniques discussed in Chapter 3, where the new product share and adoption may be modelled using the various share and adoption curve techniques presented in that chapter.

Estimating the magnitude of the effect is akin to peak share analysis – what is the change in forecast product share due to the ex-trend event?

IN-MARKET PRODUCT FORECASTING

There is one specific case of new competitor introduction for which we have good analogue data in the US – namely, the introduction of a generic product into the market. In this case, the generic product essentially is the new competitor introduced into the market. Using the share theft matrix discussed above the forecaster may readily estimate the effects of the generic introduction. In a majority of historical cases the effect of the generic product has been to gather share disproportionately from the branded product of the same active chemical composition. Use of the share theft matrix allows the forecaster to model this dynamic or, if appropriate, effects on the shares of other products in the market.

Line extensions present a unique challenge to the forecaster.

Internal ex-trend events

Internal ex-trend events are those activities under the direction of the company itself. These include activities such as the introduction of line extensions, changes in marketing strategies and programmes, and changes in sales force resource allocation. Decisions taken by the organisation regarding these activities affect future product trends.

Line extensions

Line extensions are products based on changes to currently marketed products; for example, a new dosing schedule or a new formulation of an existing product. Changing from a twice-daily dosing to once-daily dosing, or introducing an aqueous (as opposed to non-aqueous) formulation of an intranasal spray both are examples of line extensions. The goal of a line extension is to provide therapeutic benefits to the patients from the new dosing schedule or formulation. An added benefit for a company occurs when the line extension carries marketing exclusivity beyond that offered by the original formulation, or if the line extension is marketed at a higher price than the original formulation. These dynamics were discussed in detail in the cannibalisation section of Chapter 3.

The previous chapter also discussed methods for line extension forecasting, treating the line extension as a new product introduced into the market. In some cases line extensions also may be forecast using the ex-trend methodologies discussed here. If these methodologies are employed, the effect of the line extension on the in-market product is analogous to that of a new competitor entering the market and having a disproportionate effect on the currently marketed formulation. In essence, the techniques used for evaluating new competitor effects on the in-market product may be used in the forecast.

Line extensions present a unique challenge to the forecaster. The line extensions may be forecast using the new product techniques discussed in Chapter 3 or using the ex-trend and share theft matrix techniques discussed in this chapter. The choice of methodology depends upon the strategies adopted by the marketing organisation for the line extension – positioning the line extension as a new product favours new product forecasting techniques, whereas positioning the line extension to cannibalise the existing formulation leads to use of ex-trend and share theft methodologies. The fact that product positioning governs the choice of techniques is the reason line extension forecasts typically are discussed as internal ex-trend events – the timing of the introduction and positioning of the line extension are under the direction of the marketing company.

Marketing and sales activities

Changes in marketing and sales strategy and resource allocation are the primary examples of ex-trend events under control of the company. For a first-order analysis, these ex-trend events can be divided into effects due to changes in marketing (non-personal) and sales (personal) strategy and tactics. Increasingly companies are using strategies that combine non-personal and personal activities. Quantifying these second-order combined events will still use the basic principles presented in the forthcoming sections.

Marketing interventions

Marketing teams have a broad array of programmes that they can use to influence the treatment process. They may be directed at different decision-makers (for example, physicians, reimbursers, or patients). The goal of each of these programmes is to increase the decision-maker's awareness of a product and create demand for its use; however, the point at which each intervention affects the forecast variables is ubiquitous. Figure 4.5 illustrates some sample interventions and the forecast variable upon which each intervention acts. For example, direct-to-consumer advertising may drive patients to see their physician (perhaps affecting the drug-treatment rate), while disease education may affect forecast demand by enhancing patient compliance and persistence.

Changes in marketing and sales strategy and resource allocation are the primary examples of ex-trend events under control of the company.

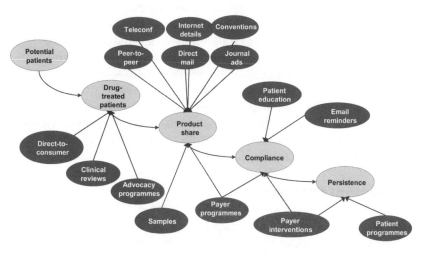

Figure 4.5   An example of the ubiquitous effects of marketing interventions

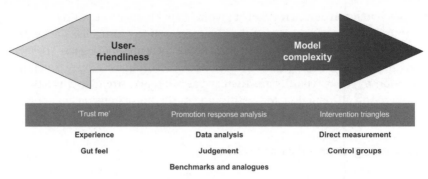

Figure 4.6 Techniques used to quantify the effects of marketing interventions

The challenge for the forecaster is to determine the quantitative effects on the forecast resulting from marketing interventions. Specifically the forecaster is concerned with changes in marketing programmes in the future from those in the past, assuming the effects of past programmes already are represented in the historical data. In Figure 4.5 interventions that affect drug-treatment rates would modify market growth, those affecting product share modify the demand for the product itself, and those interventions that affect compliance and persistence modify the prescription (or unit) to revenue conversion factors. In addition to these market variables the forecaster also needs to model effects of marketing programmes on the products themselves – for example, a marketing intervention directed at switching patients from Product A to Product B.

As with all other forecasting techniques there is a balance to strive for in the techniques employed to evaluate marketing interventions. This is demonstrated in Figure 4.6.

'Trust me'

The most user-friendly approach to quantifying ex-trend marketing interventions is the 'trust me' method. In this case the forecaster bases the quantification on prior experience and gut feel for the market. Similar to use of this technique in other forecasting exercises, the validity of the estimate is based on the knowledge and insight of the person making the judgement, and frequently lacks the transparency and defensibility of other, more analytical, techniques.

The most user-friendly approach to quantifying ex-trend marketing interventions is the 'trust me' method.

The other techniques used in quantifying marketing interventions are promotion response analysis and estimation of effects using intervention triangles. First let's discuss intervention triangles and then we will return to analysis of the promotion response.

Intervention triangles

Intervention triangles are a formalised method to capturing the magnitude and timing of a specific ex-trend marketing intervention. These data are then converted into the graph shown in Figure 4.7 – an intervention triangle.

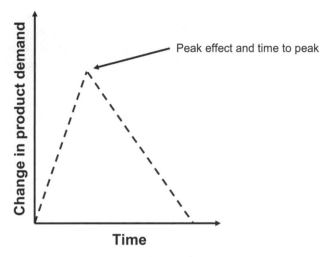

Figure 4.7   A marketing intervention triangle

This aggregate curve is termed the response curve of the product to this specific marketing programme.

There will be a unique intervention triangle generated for each marketing intervention. Every intervention triangle will contain information about the magnitude of the change (peak effect) and the timing of the change (time required to build to the peak effect and the decay of the effect over time). Typically the measurement of demand change is done in prescriptions or units and the time measurement is in months.

These individual intervention triangles may then be summed over time to obtain an aggregate response for the marketing programme. This is shown in Figure 4.8. For every time period when an intervention occurs the appropriate intervention triangle is applied. This aggregate curve is termed the *response curve* of the product to this specific marketing programme. This aggregate effect continues until the marketing intervention is stopped – at which point the effect begins to decay over time. The amount of time required for the effect to build in the market and decay depends on the shape of the intervention triangle; in some cases the effect may never decay back to its initial starting point and a legacy effect remains in the market.

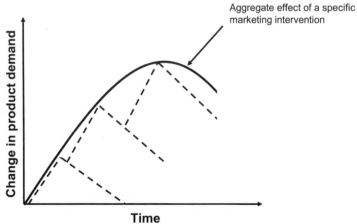

Figure 4.8   Addition of multiple intervention triangles over time

Calculating the effect of aggregate marketing interventions depends upon the shape of the intervention triangle and the timing of the intervention. This is illustrated in Table 4.3. Each of the two example interventions has the same effect – a growth in demand peaking at a gain of 100 units 3 months after the intervention takes place, followed by decay from the peak effect over time. If the second intervention is applied in time period 5 (as shown in Table 4.3) the aggregate change in demand is 70 units – 60 resulting from the 'carryover' of the first intervention and 10 resulting from the initial effect of the second intervention. Note that the aggregate effect does not have to be the smooth curve illustrated in Figure 4.8, but will have peaks and valleys that correspond to the timing of the interventions.

Table 4.3   Aggregate effect of intervention triangles

Time period	Change in demand from the first intervention	Change in demand from the second intervention	Aggregate effect
1	10	–	10
2	50	–	50
3	100	–	100
4	80	–	80
5	60	10	70
6	40	50	90
7	20	100	120
8	10	80	90
9	0	60	60
10	0	40	40
11	0	20	20
12	0	10	10

The value of response curve analysis extends beyond forecasting changes in demand.

Every marketing intervention will have its own response curve, and the shape of the curve (that is, the change in demand created by the marketing intervention) will vary among different interventions. The steeper the curve – the greater the change in demand – the more responsive the product is to that particular intervention. An intervention with a relatively flat slope (little change in demand associated with the intervention) is said to be relatively non-responsive to the marketing intervention that was modelled. These aggregate responses for all interventions are then assembled (see Figure 4.9) to provide the forecaster with a set of response curves that can be used to model the change in demand associated with a set of marketing programmes.

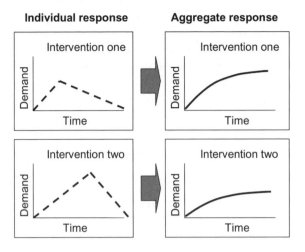

Individual response   **Aggregate response**

Intervention one

Intervention one

Intervention two

Intervention two

... and so forth for all interventions

Figure 4.9   A set of marketing intervention response curves

The value of response curve analysis extends beyond forecasting changes in demand. If the forecaster can associate costs with each intervention it is possible to calculate the return on investment for each intervention. This, in turn, allows decision-makers to prioritise the potential interventions, perhaps choosing to implement first those that yield the greatest return on investment. To calculate the return on investment the forecaster needs to know the cost of each intervention. This can be done as a simple total cost applied for an intervention (such as a patient education programme) or as a volume-related calculation (the cost for delivering a detail aid to a set number of decision-makers, calculated by multiplying the number of decision-makers by the cost per decision-maker). Once the cost parameters are applied the forecaster generates the final set of response curves, as shown in Figure 4.10.

In spite of the power of this analytical approach, forecast methods using intervention triangles are not commonly used in the pharmaceutical industry.

In spite of the power of this analytical approach, forecast methods using intervention triangles are not commonly used in the pharmaceutical industry. Why? The answer lies in the initial step of the analysis – generation of the intervention triangle. To generate this triangle the effect of the marketing

Individual response   **Aggregate response**   **Return on investment**

Intervention one

Intervention one

- Cost
- Frequency
- Penetration

Intervention one

Intervention two

Intervention two

- Cost
- Frequency
- Penetration

Intervention two

Figure 4.10   Return on investment curves for marketing interventions

programme being tested must be isolated from all other elements that can affect a change in demand. A controlled environment must be established where only the marketing intervention being examined is allowed to affect a change in demand, and the appropriate measure must be determined. The measure must be an appropriate model that isolates the effect of the marketing intervention from all other ex-trend events in the market. If a controlled market is not possible, the forecaster must be able to adjust the measure to correct for the effects of ex-trend events other than that being measured for generation of the intervention triangle.

This controlled setting is difficult to do in the pharmaceutical markets. The number of factors that affect product demand for pharmaceuticals is large – numerous marketing programmes, sales force activity, government activity, public opinion, publicity, reimbursement status, competitor marketing activities and so forth. Isolating a single variable from this mix is extremely difficult to do and is the key stumbling block to implementing marketing intervention triangles as a standard forecast method. In some cases, such as direct-to-consumer advertising in the United States, geographic test markets can be set up where only certain ads (print, television, or radio) appear. All other factors being equal (an arguable statement) the effect of the tested ad may be measured and translated into a return on investment calculation.

Given the challenges of determining intervention triangles forecasters have defaulted to the middle group – promotion response analysis. This method employs a combination of analytics and judgement to yield insights into the effectiveness of specific marketing programs and their resultant effect on a product's forecast.

Promotion response analysis

The theory behind promotion response analysis is the same as marketing intervention triangles – quantify the effects of specific marketing interventions and use the results of the analysis to forecasting the effect of future interventions. The two differences between promotion response analysis and intervention triangles are:

- promotion response analysis uses historical secondary data measures to gather quantitative insights, as opposed to the test and control groups used in intervention triangle creation; and
- promotion response analysis applies judgements to the historical data analysis to generate response curves.

The promotion response analytical approach is illustrated in Figure 4.11.

Promotion response analytics have been employed for several years in the pharmaceutical industry and there are a number of companies (and methods) used to perform the historical data analysis. Two of the often-

First, examine historical and other data for analytical insights

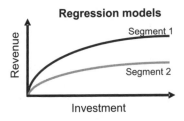

Regression models

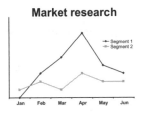

Market research

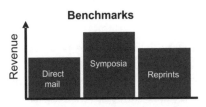

Benchmarks

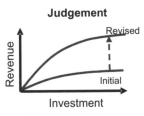

Judgement

Figure 4.11   Promotion response analysis

In the case of promotion response analysis this response curve is the result of historical data analysis, benchmarks and judgements and will be only as valid as the quality of the underlying analytics and judgements – exactly as in every other aspect of forecasting.

cited presentations in marketing mix are the *ROI Analysis of Pharmaceutical Promotion (RAPP): An Independent Study* and *Analysis of ROI for Pharmaceutical Promotion (AARP)* studies in 2001 and 2002 respectively.[2] These studies looked at a number of historical secondary data sources and suggested the return on investment obtainable in the United States though four marketing and sales interventions: detailing, direct-to-consumer advertising, medical journal advertising and physician meetings and events.

Data used in the analysis of historical promotions can be at varying levels of detail. Analysis can be done at the national level (for example, using audited country-level data) or at the individual physician level (where these data are obtainable). The advent of physician-level data in certain markets significantly enhances the ability to perform promotion mix analysis. From the more qualitative perspective, as an organisation builds internal benchmarks for promotional programmes the ability of the forecaster to use these benchmark data to support judgemental effects increases.

The challenge to promotion response analytics is the quality of the data used in the historical analysis and the quality of the judgements taken on the analytical results. The result of promotion response analysis is the same as intervention triangle analysis – a response curve for each of the marketing interventions that can be used to estimate the ex-trend effects of varying marketing interventions on the forecast. In the case of promotion response analysis this response curve is the result of historical data analysis, benchmarks and judgements and will be only as valid as the quality of the

---

2   Presentation material available at www.rxpromoroi.org.

underlying analytics and judgements – exactly as in every other aspect of forecasting.

Personal promotion activity

Changes in personal promotion activity represent the last major internal ex-trend event that the forecaster needs to quantify. In this case the ex-trend event is the change in personal promotion activity – that is, number and selling activity of the detailing (sales) representatives. The term detailing representative is used to acknowledge the activities of functions that are not directly related to sales – such as clinical liaisons, account managers and so forth. In most markets, however, personal promotion activity can be directly defined as sales force detailing activity.

The approach in quantifying the change in demand due to personal promotion activity is similar to that used in marketing interventions. The forecaster examines the changes in activity and correlates this to changes in product demand, yielding a response curve similar to that discussed for marketing interventions. In this case, however, the correlation of change in demand is to changes in personal promotion activity (see Figure 4.12). If we think of personal promotion activity in its simplest definition – number of sales representatives – we would interpret Figure 4.12 as adding additional sales representatives (increasing the value on the x-axis) in order to increase product demand (as measured on the y-axis). We would continue to add representatives until all the sales potential was exhausted (where the change in product demand becomes zero). At this point we have reached the optimal number of representatives and adding any more representatives would result in a decrease in overall profitability (since we are adding the cost of the representative, but not increasing product demand to offset this additional cost). This is the point of diminishing returns and is the theoretical maximum for personal promotion activity.

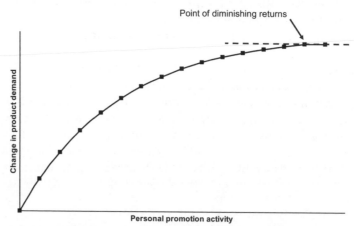

Figure 4.12 Response curve for personal promotion activity

Changes in personal promotion activity represent the last major internal ex-trend event that the forecaster needs to quantify.

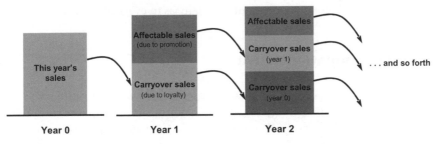

Figure 4.13 Carryover rates in personal promotion activity

There are two enhancements to the use of personal promotion response curves that augment their use in forecasting. The first is the incorporation of carryover rates (similar to the concept discussed with marketing intervention triangles); the second is better definition of what is meant by personal promotion activity.

Carryover rates reflect the dynamic of customer loyalty. From a personal promotion perspective, carryover refers to the fact that sales will be generated in future years due to the personal promotion activity in the current year – that is, customer loyalty (generated by personal promotion activity in this year) will carry over into sales in future years. This is illustrated in Figure 4.13. From the forecast perspective, the forecaster must evaluate the effect of personal promotion in the current year as well as the carryover into future years.

Carryover rates are specific to market conditions, therapeutic areas and product lifecycles. They can range from low values of 80–85 per cent to high values of 110–120 per cent. Although specific product carryover rates vary, there are some general rules that can be applied in forecasting. Carryover rates greater than 100 per cent are valid for new products where there is a tremendous amount of demand already present in the market and personal promotion activity serves as a catalyst to release the demand. Acute care products tend to have lower carryover rates than chronic care products. Products in competitive environments have lower carryover rates than products in markets with little or no competition. In estimating the ex-trend effect of a change in personal promotion activity the forecaster must estimate the carryover rate(s) for the product(s) being forecast.

Better defining personal promotion activity also leads to refinements to the ex-trend estimates used in forecasting. Referring back to Figure 4.12, the x-axis is labelled 'personal promotion activity', but this variable may be defined in several ways:

- the number of sales representatives promoting the product;
- the number of detailing representatives promoting the product (includes sales and non-sales functions);
- the amount of time spent discussing the product with the customer (referred to as detailing equivalents);

Carryover rates are specific to market conditions, therapeutic areas and product lifecycles.

IN-MARKET
PRODUCT
FORECASTING

At the end of this step of the in-market forecast algorithm the forecaster has developed the preliminary demand forecast.

	2006	2007	2008	2009	2010	2011	2012
Baseline	12,823	22,021	26,440	30,859	34,133	36,437	37,493
Ex-trend event 1	-13	-1,899	-2,640	-3,086	-3,413	-3,644	-3,749
Ex-trend event 2		-617	-1,053	-1,234	-1,365	-1,457	-1,500
Ex-trend event 3					-8,873	-12,746	-13,123
Preliminary demand forecast	12,810	19,504	22,747	26,539	20,481	18,590	17,975

Figure 4.14 Preliminary demand forecast with trend and ex-trend analyses

- segmentation of the customer group – for example, creating different response curves for physician specialties;
- separating promotion activity into the reach into the customer segment, and the frequency or number of times an individual customer receives a personal promotion visit; and
- measuring the effectiveness of personal promotion activity and using an effectiveness measure on the x-axis.

As sales force strategy has evolved over time the refinement of personal promotion activity has increased from the beginning of the above list, moving towards the effectiveness measures towards the bottom of the list. The forecaster needs to be concerned about which measure is used for personal promotion activity because it is changes in this measure that must be translated into the ex-trend effect on product revenue.

Preliminary demand forecast

At the end of this step of the in-market forecast algorithm the forecaster has developed the preliminary demand forecast. This forecast is based first on trending of the historical data and then on applying the effects of ex-trend events. An example of a typical forecast output at this stage is shown in Figure 4.14. This forecast reflects modifications to the historical data used in trending product demand. In the next section we will discuss corrections for demand channels other than those measured in the historical data, modifications due to distributor activity and corrections for activities such as parallel importation.

CONVERTING TRENDED DATA INTO FORECAST OUTPUTS

Once the trend and ex-trend events have been quantified the forecaster is ready to convert this preliminary forecast into a revenue forecast. This is represented by the 'reconciliation and conversion' section of the algorithm in Figure 4.1. This section consists of two major steps: reconciling the demand forecast to the ex-factory forecast, and converting ex-factory units to ex-factory revenue.

Channel corrections

If a product is dispensed in both retail pharmacies and hospitals, but only data related to retail pharmacy demand were used in the trend and ex-trend analyses, the forecaster would have ignored the demand in the hospital sector in the previous steps of the in-market forecast algorithm. In this example, the retail channel would have been forecast, but the hospital channel would have been ignored. 'Channel corrections' refers to the inclusion of demand in those channels not captured in the underlying trending and ex-trend analysis. Channels not captured in the underlying dataset often are referred to as 'unaudited channels'.

The identity of unaudited channels differs by country, by therapy area and by product. Potential unaudited channels include hospitals, nursing homes, long-term care facilities, mail-order, Internet pharmacy, government dispensing, physician offices, treatment centres (such as dialysis centres and oncology clinics) and any other direct distributors who do not report into one of the data capture companies. For some of these channels data may be available, and the forecaster can analyse demand in these channels as described in the previous sections of this chapter. Therefore, it is not uncommon to have a trend plus ex-trend forecast for each audited channel (retail, hospital, mail order and so forth) and to then apply the corrections for unaudited channels.

Take Figure 4.15 as an example of the data for three products to be forecast. The shaded cells in the table represent the data available through audits and other data sources. The unshaded cells contain estimates of volume for those particular channels, but no historical dataset exists for these unaudited channels.

In this example the forecaster would use the data from the audited channels (shaded cells) to create the preliminary demand forecast. This would be based on trending of the underlying data plus the effects of ex-trend events. For products A and B the preliminary demand forecast would consist of a single dataset. For product C, however, there would be three preliminary trend plus ex-trend forecasts; one for each of the three audited channels. For all products the forecaster would then add the correction for unaudited channels

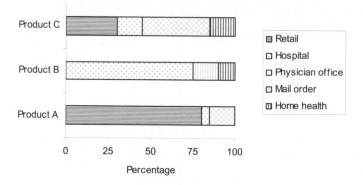

Percentage of volume by channel and product

Channel	Product A	Product B	Product C
Retail	80	0	30
Hospital	5	75	15
Physician office	0	15	0
Mail order	15	0	40
Home health	0	10	15

Note: historical data available for shaded cells; others are estimates

Figure 4.15   An example of products with audited and unaudited channels

in order to get to the true demand forecast. For product A this would consist
of bulking up the preliminary forecast by 20 per cent to account for the
unaudited demand (5 per cent in the hospital channel and 15 per cent in
mail order). Similarly the preliminary demand forecast for product B would be
increased by 25 per cent and the preliminary demand forecast for product C
increased by 15 per cent.

Once the unaudited channel demand has been added to the preliminary
demand forecast a true demand forecast has been created. This demand
forecast represents the product that will be consumed by the end-user. This
does not, however, represent the product that must be supplied by the
manufacturer. There exists another market dynamic that occurs between the
manufacturer and the end-user – that of product distribution.

Distributor activity

There exists another market dynamic that occurs between the manufacturer and the end user – that of product distribution.

Distributors play an intermediary role between the pharmaceutical
manufacturer and the end-user of the product. For example, a wholesaler may
purchase product from the pharmaceutical manufacturer, ship it to numerous
retail pharmacies, which then dispense the product to the consumer when
filling a prescription. In this case there are two distributors involved – the
large wholesaler and the retail pharmacy. Both distributors purchase product
and hold it in inventory on their shelves until the product is needed in the
market (either to fill the retail pharmacy's order to the wholesaler, or to fill
the consumer's prescription at the retail pharmacy).

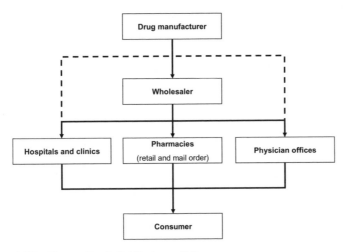

Figure 4.16 Generalised distributor activity

Other distribution channels include entities such as hospitals, clinics, physician offices, treatment centres and so forth. The exact nature of the distributors depends upon the country being considered and the therapy area involved. For example, some products that are used primarily in the hospital may be shipped directly from the manufacturer to the hospital, instead of using a wholesaler as the primary distribution point. A generalised distribution channel diagram is shown in Figure 4.16. Using the solid arrows to indicate the primary distribution channels and the dashed arrows to indicate secondary distribution channels, this diagram suggests the majority of product flow move through wholesalers and pharmacies, with a secondary flow through hospitals and physician offices. Each therapy area and product to be forecast will have a different emphasis on the arrows to indicate different volume flows.

This dynamic creates a significant challenge for the forecaster. The amount of product being held in inventory by the distributors creates disparity between the ex-factory sales (what the manufacturer sells to the distributor) and product demand (what is dispensed to the consumer). This creates two types of forecasts – an ex-factory sales forecast and a true product demand forecast. The difference between the two is due to inventory levels held by the distributors. This is illustrated in Figure 4.17.

Figure 4.17 illustrates several important distributor dynamics that affect the forecast (both demand and ex-factory sales). These are timing, pipeline fill and bleed and speculation.

Timing

Differences in timing between recognition of the ex-factory shipments and demand measured at the consumer level create the data patterns in Figure 4.17. Data related to consumer demand are smoother than ex-factory shipment data. Consumer demand is measured as each unit is dispensed,

*The challenge
to the forecaster
is to project the
initial pipeline fill
quantities.*

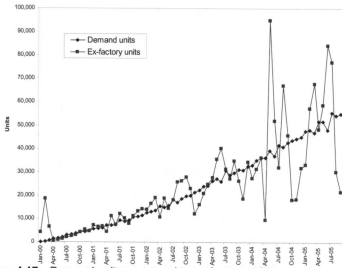

Figure 4.17 Demand units compared to ex-factory units

creating a measurement based on growth of a large number of smaller units dispensed (for example, single prescriptions of 30 tablets). Ex-factory shipments are recorded as large numbers of units are sent to the distributor (for example, thousands of bottles of 500 tablets). This creates a less uniform pattern of product shipments – greater volume as orders are shipped, then a lull in ex-factory shipments as these units are dispensed to meet consumer demand, then another large shipment, and so forth. This gives rise to the swings associated with the ex-factory units shipped as seen in Figure 4.16. As ex-factory units shipped are converted to revenue recognised by the manufacturer, this creates the same peaks and valleys of product sales.

Pipeline fill and bleed

Pipeline fill and bleed refers to the distribution activity when a product is first introduced into the market, as shown in Figure 4.18. There is a large spike in the ex-factory units shipped at product introduction in order to fill the distributors' pipelines – that is, to stock their shelves with the inventory needed to meet consumer demand. As product demand rises, this initial inventory level is worked off until the distributor reaches an ongoing inventory level – ranging from two to four weeks of projected product demand. This dynamic of depleting initial inventory levels until an ongoing level is reached is referred to as product bleed.

The challenge to the forecaster is to project the initial pipeline fill quantities. This represents the initial shipment of units required to fill the distributors' pipelines. Historically this value has been estimated as a multiple of ongoing demand levels – for example, twice the number of units expected to meet consumer demand six months after launch. For products that have short manufacturing lead times and/or long shelf lives the pipeline fill forecast is not critical. For products that have long lead times and/or very short shelf

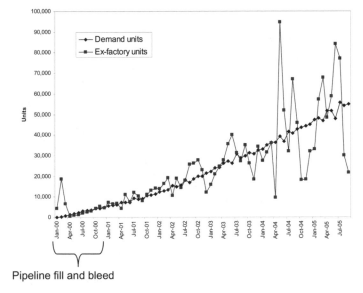

Pipeline fill and bleed

Figure 4.18 Pipeline fill and bleed

lives this pipeline fill forecast becomes more important – a wrong forecast can lead to a back order of product (if the forecast demand was less than actual demand) or to losses through destroyed goods (if the forecast demand was higher than actual demand and product needed to be destroyed due to shelf life expiry).

The dynamics of pipeline fill also can lead to questionable financial reporting. Once the product is shipped from the manufacturer to the distributor the sale is recognised and the revenue recorded. If a situation occurs where the manufacturer overloads the distribution channel higher than normal revenues would be recorded for the product. For example, if the distributor has an incentive to hold higher-than-expected initial inventory levels the manufacturer would record higher-than-expected revenues for the product. Distributor incentives can include things such as stocking fees paid to the distributor to stock the product on their shelves or a significant increase in the amount of time before a distributor must pay the manufacturer for the product. This dynamic is referred to as channel stuffing and to the extent that this misleads investors it is an illegal activity in some countries.

Speculation

The dynamic of product speculation is shown in the right section of Figure 4.19. In this part of the graph the peaks and valleys associated with ex-factory shipments to the distributor are magnified from prior years. This is an indicator of speculation. Speculation occurs in markets where the pharmaceutical manufacturer takes price increases and the distributor speculates on the time and magnitude of the price increase. If the distributor purchases product from the manufacturer *before* a price increase and then sells it to the consumer *after* the price increase, the distributor makes a profit from

Speculation occurs in markets where the pharmaceutical manufacturer takes price increases and the distributor speculates on the time and magnitude of the price increase.

IN-MARKET
PRODUCT
FORECASTING

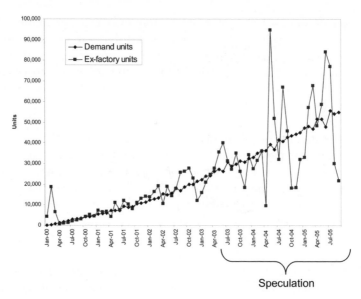

Figure 4.19 Speculation

the speculation. For example, if a distributor buys product in April valued at €100,000, and the manufacturer takes a 5 per cent price increase effective May 1, the distributor can then sell the product at €105,000 (at a 5 per cent higher price) to obtain a profit of €5,000. This is profit arising simply from speculation of price increases and purchasing product from the manufacturer prior to the announced price increase.

For the manufacturer, however, there are few – if any – advantages to speculation.

The distributor wishes to speculate as much as possible. Speculation is a relatively easy way to increase distributor profits. The only cost to the distributor in speculating is the space required to hold the purchased product and the upfront payment to the manufacturer for the purchased goods. If the manufacturer offers terms – that is, the manufacturer does not require payment from the distributor until 30–90 days past the purchase date – the distributor does not even need the upfront payment to the manufacturer. In this case the only barrier to speculation is the space required to hold product, and this usually is a fixed overhead cost to the distributor that does not significantly increase with purchased product volumes. In essence, there are no real barriers to the distributor in speculating, and there can be significant financial advantages.

For the manufacturer, however, there are few – if any – advantages to speculation. As the distributor purchases large volumes for speculation the disparity between ex-factory shipments and true demand grows (as shown in Figure 4.19). Factory shipments become driven by speculation behaviour of the distributors. The units – and revenue – reported by the manufacturer become more erratic and less reflective of consumer product demand. This makes forecasting of ex-factory units and revenues more difficult because the forecaster must not only model product demand, but also estimate the degree of speculation by the distributors.

Speculation occurs when the value gained from price increases in the market creates the financial incentive for the distributor to speculate. In markets where price increases are small and/or the timing is pre-determined speculation is not as much of a concern. One of the major markets where speculation has, and continues to be a major concern, is the United States (US).

There is an intriguing history of distributor–manufacturer dynamics in the US pharmaceutical market. Speculation first appeared at a significant level in the US markets in the 1980s, when price increases typically were higher than inflation. There is no set schedule for price increases for pharmaceutical products and manufacturers can take a price increase at their discretion. This led to speculative behaviour by the distributors, primarily wholesalers in the US market.

Once speculation began in the US markets the manufacturers were faced with the disparities between ex-factory shipments and demand data. In order to quell speculation manufacturers first offered wholesalers the ability to purchase product at the old price for a period of time after a price increase was announced. The theory behind this 'buy-in' was to allow wholesalers to buy at the old price and resell at the new, higher price without the wholesaler needing to speculate. If the wholesaler could purchase product at the old price after a price increase was announced, there would be no need for the wholesaler to speculate and purchase large quantities of product prior to the price increase. Buy-in terms usually were extended for one to two months after the price increase was announced. In theory, this would smooth the ex-factory sales shipments because wholesalers would not need to speculate.

What was the result? The manufacturers did not see the smoothing of ex-factory shipments as they hoped. Instead, they saw speculation shift from before the price increase was taken to after the price increase was taken. The theory behind the speculation behaviour remained the same – the wholesaler could still purchase large quantities of product at the old price and resell it at the new, higher price. Only the timing changed. Now instead of creating a surge in product purchased prior to the price increase the wholesaler simply purchased a large volume of product in the post-price increase period, and still resold it at the higher price.

The manufacturers responded to this wholesaler behaviour by limiting the amount of product the wholesaler could purchase at the old price. They created terms for the buy-in that limited the amount of product the wholesaler could purchase at the old price, typically linked to the volume purchased by the wholesaler prior to the price increase. What was the effect of applying terms to the buy-in? It simply shifted the speculation behaviour back to the pre-price period. If the wholesaler was limited in the buy-in period to a multiple of the volume before the price increase was taken, the wholesaler simply purchased more product in this pre-price increase period. This increased the volume the wholesaler could purchase (at the old price) in the post-price increase period, and created a greater financial gain for the wholesaler through speculation.

In short, there are no simple activities the manufacturer can take to diminish distributor speculation by regulating volumes. Attempts to diminish speculation simply shift the speculation period. Manufacturers can take the ultimate step and stop shipments to the distributors to stop speculation and force the distributors to diminish their inventories, but this is a short-sighted solution that could potentially result in product shortages to the end consumer. For a pharmaceutical product this has far-reaching consequences on a patient's health and physician trust in continuous supply in the future.

Instead of these draconian measures manufacturers are now starting to 'partner' with distributors to diminish the need for speculation behaviour. The onus is on the manufacturer to offer incentives to the distributor such that the distributor does not need to engage in speculation. These incentives usually are referred to as 'inventory management agreements' between the manufacturer and the distributor. In the US market the terms of these agreements are proprietary but presumably offer advantages to both the manufacturer and the distributor (wholesaler).

In summary, the forecaster is challenged because of the disparity between consumer demand data and ex-factory shipment data. To the extent that speculation occurs in the market the forecaster must project the behaviour of the distributor in purchasing product. This correction for distributor purchasing behaviour must be applied to the underlying consumer demand forecast in order to generate an ex-factory unit and revenue forecast.

Parallel imports

Parallel imports – also called grey-market imports – are products produced under the protection of a trademark or patent in one market (country), and then imported into a second market (country) without the authorisation of the local owner of the intellectual property right. For example, it is permissible for a parallel importer (repackager) to purchase quantities of prescription drugs in Spain and import them into the UK or Germany without the approval of the local manufacturer who owns the licensed patent rights. In fact, rules of the internal market in the European Union permit parallel trade among those countries. A schematic showing product flow when parallel imports are involved is shown in Figure 4.20.

Whereas parallel importation is common in the European Union it is not common in the United States due to two legal constraints. First, US patent owners are protected from parallel imports by an explicit right of importation. Second, parallel import of trademarked prescription drugs is explicitly excluded under terms of a 1988 law covering pharmaceuticals. It should be noted that this does not apply to re-sale of drugs within the US; therefore, Internet sales of pharmaceutical products is not considered parallel

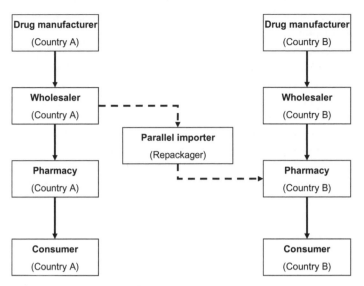

Figure 4.20 An illustration of parallel imports

importation if the product was originally sold in the US and then repackaged by the Internet seller. The Internet seller is simply another distribution channel in this case.

Japan allows parallel importation in patented and trademarked goods unless the goods are explicitly barred by contract provision or unless their original sale was subject to foreign price regulation. Japan is more open to parallel importation than the US, but less open than the EU. Australia generally permits parallel imports in trademarked goods, but patent owners may block them; therefore, Australia is not a large market for parallel importation. (For a more detailed discussion of parallel importation and its legal and regulatory background see Maskus.[3])

One recent exception to these general observations for the US market is the rise of cross-border movement of pharmaceutical products between Canada and the US. One of the motivating factors for parallel importation is a difference in price between products. For several pharmaceutical products the price in Canada is below that in the US. Beginning in 2004 there were reports of people living near the US–Canadian border travelling to Canada to have their prescriptions filled and then returning to the US. In this case the product crosses borders with the individual.

One of the motivating factors for parallel importation is a difference in price between products.

What is the challenge for the forecaster? It is a similar challenge to that noted previously in the disparity between ex-factory sales and market demand. Referring to Figure 4.20, the manufacturer in Country A recognises the sale to the wholesaler in Country A, but the units are dispensed and recorded in

3   Maskus, K. E. (2001) *Parallel Imports in Pharmaceuticals: Implications for Competition and Prices in Developing Countries*. Available at www.wipo.int/about-ip/en/studies/pdf/ssa-maskus__pi.pdf# search='maskus%20parallel%20imports'.

IN-MARKET
PRODUCT
FORECASTING

Country B. The movement through the parallel importer creates the disparity between ex-factory sales and market demand.

In the country where the product originated, ex-factory sales will be inflated relative to product demand in that country. In the country where the product was imported, ex-factory sales will be lower than that suggested by product demand within that country. For example, in the Spain to UK example cited in the first paragraph of this section, the ex-factory sales in Spain would be higher than forecast from demand in the Spanish market, while sales in the UK would be lower than expected from demand in the UK. The forecaster must correct for the level of parallel importation in both the exporting and importing markets. As with other elements in the reconciliation and conversion part of the in-market algorithm, these corrections are country, therapy area and product-specific. The general guiding principle is that the greater the price disparity between markets the greater the level of parallel importation (where legally allowed).

FINAL CONSIDERATIONS

The greatest challenge to the forecaster for in-market products is in the conversion of the demand forecast into an ex-factory sales forecast.

The chapter considered approaches to in-market product forecasting, beginning with treatment of historical data and then applying the quantification of ex-trend event to reach a preliminary demand forecast for the product. This preliminary forecast is then adjusted for unaudited channels, distributor activity and corrections for parallel imports where appropriate. As with all forecasting exercises, the forecaster combines data and judgement to yield a forecast. In the case of in-market products the judgements of the forecast are often hidden from the end-user of the forecast – for example, the number of historical datapoints selected for trend analysis. To aid in forecast transparency these judgements need to be visible to the user of the forecast.

The greatest challenge to the forecaster for in-market products is in the conversion of the demand forecast into an ex-factory sales forecast. This challenge arises because of dynamics in the distribution channel, where the distributor can create disparities between product demand and ex-factory shipments due to their purchasing activity. This activity – out of the control and often out of awareness of the pharmaceutical manufacturer – remains the most difficult element of in-market forecasting.

CHAPTER 5

Thoughts for the Future

I always hesitate to make predictions, especially when it involves the future.

Mark Twain

I think the greatest error in forecasting is not realizing how important are the probabilities of events other than those everyone is agreeing upon.

Paul Samuelson

The preceding chapters of this text discussed the challenges of forecasting and the approaches a forecaster may take in meeting these challenges. This chapter applies these learnings inwardly, and offers a forecast on the future of forecasting. Where is the pharmaceutical industry headed with forecasting in the future?

ERA OF REVITALISATION

One of the tenets of in-market forecasting is that there is knowledge to be gained from a review of the historical data. By examining history we gain insights into product performance and product response to various external (ex-trend) events. What can we learn from the same retrospective analysis of forecasting?

Forecasting has evolved over time as the environment has changed (see Table 5.1). In the 1970s the pharmaceutical markets were relatively uncomplicated, and complex strategic planning was not needed. In the 1980s a burgeoning global economy and relatively few restrictions on pharmaceutical pricing led to accelerating product growth. Once again the need for forecasting was low as companies basked in their commercial success.

Where is the pharmaceutical industry headed with forecasting in the future?

Table 5.1   Forecasting eras

1970s	Age of unplanning
1980s	Delusions of grandeur
1990s	Age of disappointment
2000s	Era of revitalisation

In the early 1990s pressures on the pharmaceutical industry began to increase. Contraction in economies, pressure on pharmaceutical prices, increasing competitive pressure and loss of marketing exclusivity on major products drove the need for more accurate planning and forecasting. Coming from a history of low need for forecasting, the industry struggled to develop the science of forecasting and disappointment resulted from the industry's inexperience in this area.

The late 1990s and the beginning of the twenty-first century saw a growth in the application and sophistication of forecasting. In response to commercial pressure on the industry, strategic planning for the future took on greater importance and forecasting became a major contributor to the strategic planning function. In response to this need, the tools and methods available to the forecaster became more sophisticated and the ability to model various strategic options was now viable.

This resurgence continues today. Forecasting has become a keystone in future planning functions such as strategic planning, business development and portfolio optimisation. The processes, tools and methods available to the forecaster have continued to develop and contribute actively to the revitalisation of the forecasting function.

The role of the forecaster also has evolved over time and continues to evolve into the future. In forward-thinking organisations the forecasting position is no longer one of simple spreadsheet manipulation; rather, the forecaster has evolved into a holistic painter of the future.

Forecasting has become a keystone in future planning functions such as strategic planning, business development and portfolio optimisation.

CREATE STORIES, NOT SPREADSHEETS

In the Introduction we asked 'What is a forecast?' and listed a number of potential answers to this question. In subsequent chapters we discussed the processes, tools, methods and analytics available to the forecaster to answer this question. As we saw, these are varied – reflecting the multiple demands upon a forecast by the functional areas within an organisation. In spite of this variance, every answer involved two basic concepts – achieveing a balance between user-friendliness and technical complexity, and exposing decision-makers to the uncertainty in the forecast numbers.

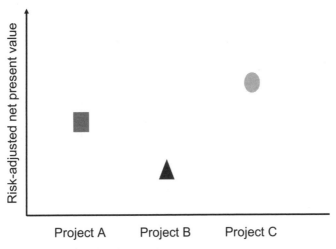

Figure 5.1 Comparing project alternatives

In this concluding chapter we pose a slightly different question – 'What is the job of a forecaster?' One of the most prevalent answers is 'to predict the future accurately'. This is but a partial answer. As we have seen, the job of a forecaster is more expansive – to create a logical framework in which future events can be quantitatively evaluated. The job of the forecaster is to create stories that paint an holistic picture of the future, not simply spreadsheets.

This can be illustrated by a simple example. Consider three projects, whose point forecast returns to the company (as measured by risk-adjusted net present value) are shown in Figure 5.1. Project C has the highest risk-adjusted net present value and would be preferred over the other projects.

The decision, however, becomes less clear when the uncertainty ranges also are presented with each point estimate, as shown in Figure 5.2. Would you select Project C – which has a higher average risk-adjusted net present value, but little upside potential and significant downside risk – or Project A, which has a lower point estimate than Project C, but has higher upside potential and lower downside risk. There is no clear answer; the selection would depend upon the risk profile of the decision-makers and the corporate tolerance for risk.

How can the forecaster help in the decision-making? By communicating the 'story' behind each product forecast and not simply the point forecast. What is leading to the uncertainty? Can any of the uncertainty be resolved in the planning process? How were the uncertainty ranges determined? What is causing the average value for Project C to tend towards the high side of the uncertainty range? These are the key questions the decision-makers must ask, and the forecaster is in the position to better inform the decision-makers through each product's story.

The story being told by the forecaster may be as simple as the example above, or may be a more complex vision of the future. In this latter approach the

THOUGHTS FOR
THE FUTURE

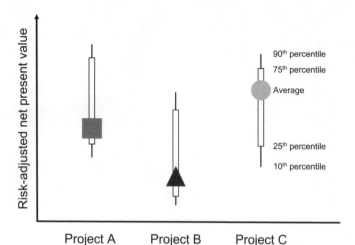

Figure 5.2   Comparing project alternatives with uncertainty ranges

forecaster develops different scenarios of the future and evaluates product performance (and uncertainty) in each of these alternative futures.

HIRE A SCIENCE FICTION WRITER

As Michael Schrage suggested in his provocative comment about 'hiring one good science fiction writer', the key to strategic forecasting is thinking about possible futures so that a company may better plan for the future.[1] Although science fiction writers may find it difficult to contribute directly to pharmaceutical forecasting, the concept of alternative futures is used increasingly in strategic forecasting.

What are 'alternative futures?' This concept, sometimes referred to as game theory or war games, allows an organisation to evaluate different strategies for the future. The forecaster is already adept at drawing insights from historical data, capturing expert judgement, and evaluating these effects in structural modelling. By coupling identification of different scenarios in the future – alternative futures – with these skills, the forecaster can enable more strategic decision-making in organisations (see Figure 5.3).

The key to strategic forecasting is thinking about possible futures so that a company may better plan for the future.

HOLISTIC FORECASTING

In Chapter 1 we discussed the role of forecasts in driving decision-making across a variety of different functional areas. In Chapter 2 we presented a set of processes, tools, and methods with which the forecaster can create more insightful forecasts. In Chapters 3 and 4 these methods were applied to new product and in-market forecasting.

---

1   Schrage, M. (1991) 'Spreadsheets Paper Over Real Problems', *Los Angeles Times*, 11 April, part D, p. 1.

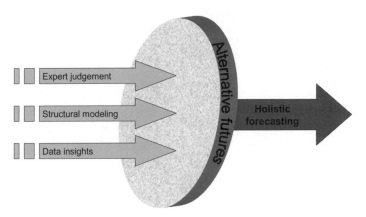

Figure 5.3　The future of forecasting

The integration of these concepts – diverse decision-makers, sophisticated methods, broad relevance, and strategic application – creates tremendous value and competitive advantage for an organisation. The future of forecasting is its transformation from simple number reporting to offering these holistic frameworks in which to evaluate potential futures.

The future of forecasting is its transformation from simple number reporting to offering these holistic frameworks in which to evaluate potential futures.

CHAPTER 6

PharmaCo – A Forecasting Case Study

TUESDAY

Anna Nitschneider stepped out of the fifth floor elevator, glanced a quick smile at the executive secretary and rounded the corner towards the boardroom. She felt prepared for this morning's meeting with the Vice-President of Marketing and Sales. She readjusted her grip on her laptop briefcase, cleared her throat and quietly passed though the double walnut doors of the meeting room.

'We have some new ideas about the product forecasts that we'd like you to have a look at.'

Promoted to Forecasting Director six months prior, Anna had been with PharmaCo's sales division for almost a decade. As a star sales representative, she had worked her way up to District Manager of San Francisco South. Years of sales experience had developed in her a good intuitive sense about marketing strategy and how a product was likely to perform, but she found forecasting to be a bit more quantitative than what she was used to. It was now her task to forecast the market performance of compounds in PharmaCo's product pipeline, and to project the future revenues of products that had recently been launched and had some historical sales data behind them. Yesterday after lunch she had received the email summoning her to this morning's meeting, but the details were unclear. Brian Nolan, the Vice-President of Marketing and Sales, had made it short and to the point, writing 'We have some new ideas about the product forecasts that we'd like you to have a look at.'

After an affirmative 'Hello, good morning everyone', Anna situated herself across the table from the marketing team with her back to the windows. Before her was a packet emblazoned with the tricolor PharmaCo logo and a heading which read, 'Product Portfolio Forecast 2006'. Then Brian Nolan began, 'Good morning, Anna. Sorry about the short notice, but as you know, we're in a bit of a transition phase right now and things are moving along pretty rapidly. We're thinking of advancing the launch date of Orthonova, and we're still not sure how Verdantin's going to perform after expiration. But that's only the tip of the iceberg. So I'd like to get things out in the open right off the bat – Anna, we want you to run a forecast for the whole portfolio. So that includes Orthonova, Cytoflux, and the others as well.'

'What's our timeline on this?' asked Anna, maintaining eye contact as she reached for her briefcase to retrieve a pen.

'Three months,' barked the triangular conferencing phone from the centre of the table. It was Jennifer Knighton, PharmaCo's CEO. 'Consider this your new priority Anna. I want you to get a forecast team together and have some results for us by April. Can you handle this?'

'Yes,' she replied quickly. 'I can do it.'

'Great! I'll let Brian brief you on the details. Good luck.' The call ended with a sharp click. Anna looked back at Brian Nolan with her lips parted and her right brow slightly cocked.

'Excellent. Shall we?' asked Nolan taking up his packet in both hands and stacking the sheets together several times to make the edges even. Anna followed suit, already brainstorming the data requests she would need to deliver to the various Product Managers, Market Research Managers, and Analysts later that day.

WEDNESDAY

Anna plugged in her laptop again at 07:30. She checked email thinking to herself, 'Who could have sent anything between eleven last night and now?' Nothing but a health club membership upgrade message. Delete. She straightened up and opened her 'to do' list and reviewed the agenda she had compiled the night before.

She was especially concerned with modelling factors surrounding demand for Cytoflux. Anna needed to create a production forecast that was close to the distributors' actual needs. To do this, she had to reconcile the difference between the demand forecast (like the one she was about to perform for Ortho) and the actual shipment numbers for which Brian Nolan was asking. She had some data for two distribution channels – retail and hospital – that covered about 95 per cent of all Cytoflux sales in 2003–2005. She needed to use these numbers to arrive at an adjusted demand forecast for 2006. That seemed to be the easy part – it was just a matter of looking at the historical data to identify a trend from which she could extrapolate the demand. She knew the data sources well enough to know that demand data projections were not a full census and would likely need a bulk-up factor applied to them. Tack on a standard percentage for the inventory pipeline in the early months and she would be there. When she reviewed the Cytoflux data, she furrowed her brow and tried to stem the rising tide of stress. It was times like this when the urge to escape to the Evian vending machine in the side room off the lobby became fitfully tempting. 'Time crunch,' she repressed herself. Back to the task, she tried to make sense of the jagged lines and bars on the chart from Nolan (see Exhibit 2). After a few minutes of figuring, Anna added another item to her 'to do' list and turned back to the packet from Tuesday's meeting.

She turned to the launch of Orthonova, which was expected to be the most significant source of revenue for PharmaCo in the near to mid-future. Nolan had stressed in yesterday's meeting that the production process was going to be more expensive than they had previously thought because of an added refinement step. He had specifically asked her to prepare a production needs report by the end of the week so that they could get a better handle on the budget requirements over the next quarter. 'We really, really need an accurate forecast', echoed in her mind.

She went to her project drive and opened the file labelled Patient-based_ Ortho_Forecast. All she had to do now was convert the patient numbers to product volume, but how? 'Let's see,' she thought to herself. 'I know that Orthonova is once daily, and patients take it every day. How many pills is that?' Luckily, she had some data for days of therapy for a competing product, Cartilin, which she could use for Orthonova. From there, she could get to compliance, and from compliance, she could get to product volume (see Exhibits 3.1 and 3.2).

In addition to these production exercises, Nolan had expressed concern over a mysterious trend in Verdantin's TRx levels over the past year and a half. 'Look at this graph Anna. We have the new indication coming out on Verdy but I'm worried about this trend. You can see that more and more patients are being treated for depression and they should be on our drug, but they're not. The TRx numbers are dropping. I don't know if this is because generics are on the horizon or what. Take Cytoflux, Anna. It's doing the opposite thing. Look at this – the dollar sales are going up faster that the TRxes. If only we could get all our products to do that!' She turned to the graphs in her packet and considered phoning their data vendor to see if he could pull some quick data by tomorrow morning. At the same time, she wondered whether Nolan was right about Cytoflux. She seemed to think that comparing the trends between Cyto and Verdy was like comparing apples and oranges. 'Yeah, I'd better give our data vendor a call,' she thought (see Exhibits 4 and 5).

'We really, really need an accurate forecast'.

Upon finishing lunch, Anna discovered an email that Kerre Wood from market research had bounced up with some data she wanted, except for one piece. Yesterday after the meeting, she requested that the market research team compile a list of the current products in the osteoarthritis market environment along with their respective shares. She also wanted them to include the results from the uptake curve she had them generate a week earlier. Finally, she had asked the team to assess the amount of share that Orthonova would be expected to take from each competitor product.

Why wouldn't prescriptions follow days of therapy?

Kerre explained, 'We came up with a couple of ways to calculate the share that Orthonova's going to take from each competitor, but we figured you'd be the best one to decide. I pasted the tables underneath the uptake curve. Regards, Kerre.' Anna took a sip of her non-fat vanilla latte and clicked open the Excel attachment at the bottom of Kerre's email. She nodded her head and organised her thoughts as her eyes scanned the tables. In addition to the share theft analysis, she noted that Kerre had left her adoption pattern intact. She was pleased to learn that the market research group concurred with her belief that, in light of its novel mechanism of action and anticipated aggressive promotion, the Orthonova uptake pattern was likely to parallel that of Lipitor. At the bottom of the attachment was another note which read, 'Note that Osteoarthritis TRxes have increased over the past two years, but days of therapy (DOTs) have lagged. Important?' Underneath was a graph displaying the trend. Why wouldn't prescriptions follow days of therapy? Probably something to look into (see Exhibit 6).

Anna returned to the office after meeting her friend Lee for dinner across the street. She sat down at her computer and cancelled sleep mode. With a beep and bright flash, the flat screen came to life again, displaying the cannibalisation table for Verdantin that she had been constructing before dinner. She was trying to find out how many patients on the current formulation will be stolen away when they release the once-weekly in six months (see Exhibit 7). She pulled a similar table for Listromycin from the project archives (Exhibit 8). Listro was one of the drugs that helped make PharmaCo successful throughout the first part of the 2000s. Now off patent, its market share was all but residual since the generics had moved in. Anna looked it over briefly because it was similar in construction to the cannibalisation table. Across the hall, Nancy Weber, one of PharmaCo's marketing analysts turned off the light in her office and pushed in her swivel chair. 'Working late again, Anna?' she asked, hoisting her bag strap higher up on her shoulder.

'You know it,' replied Anna in a monotone voice, her gaze fixed on the screen.

'Don't work *too* hard! Goodnight.'

THURSDAY

'Anna, hi. I just wanted to see where we stand after the meeting on Tuesday.'

'I've done some things on the in-markets, Brian, and now I'm focusing on the pre-launch products. Things are looking good.'

'Excellent. I've got a meeting in Boston tomorrow, so I'll be out until Monday. Just let Steve know if anything comes up. Good?'

'Sure, Brian. Talk to you later.' Anna hung up the phone and turned back to the epidemiology data she had tabulated from several literature searches. She was looking at a plot she had generated from diagnosis rates for osteoarthritis, and even though the rates had been growing steadily over the past few years, the total number of drug-treated patients was decreasing. Furthermore, epidemiology sources revealed that a percentage of the population afflicted with the disease remained undiagnosed (see Exhibit 10). She had some theories about why this could be; some suggested that it could be a problem for the upcoming launch of Orthonova. Anna also had to perform a complete forecast of Orthonova to prepare for the launch strategy. Last week she had met with a number of individuals from the marketing team to draft an agenda for this task. They had come to a sticking point when Kerre Wood suggested using a patient-based model. Ruth Brentari, a former district manager like Anna, felt that it would be better to use a prescription-based model. During the argument, Anna tried to sort out the pros and cons of each approach. She had to make up her mind soon, because she intended to put either Kerre or Ruth on the forecast team, but not both.

In that meeting, they had also discussed the different methods they could use to estimate Orthonova's market share forecast. This part of the discussion was a bit more collaborative, because they could all agree that relying on gut feel was too inaccurate. It was quick and dirty, and that meant inexpensive, but they knew from experience that better data sources were out there. Another problem was that Brad Thomas had retired last fall. He used to be the go-to man for intuition on this sort of thing. That being said, Brad's gut feel didn't always prove best in retrospect.

Two other methods of estimating market share were placed on the table and the group had decided to list the pros and cons of each – somewhat of a qualitative cost–benefit analysis. The first method measured the peak share and the time it would take to reach that level. The second method, attribute scoring, was a bit more complicated. Anna had experience with attribute scoring, so she was the most prepared to give input about it. They took about an hour to discuss the two methods, and now she sat at her desk looking at some of her notes from that meeting (Exhibit 10).

Brad's gut feel didn't always prove best in retrospect.

Anna was being cautious about how they were going to proceed with the forecasts because of problems PharmaCo had had in the past when they forecast pre-launch products. Back when she took the forecasting directorship, the first thing she did was to review some archived files to get a feel for the existing methodology. What she found was often puzzling. About a week into the job, she had pulled a market share projection graph for Cytoflux that marketing had generated back in 2000 – right before launch. She overlaid that graph with a plot depicting what had actually happened in 2001 after the launch, and the results were revealing (Exhibit 11). Even though the projection for share after the first year was close to the real number, the road getting there was completely different. Apparently, Cytoflux historically had been difficult to model. Later on, she had found another Excel chart that displayed patient number projections back in 2001. They had expected the number of patients to stay steady up to 2005. The audited numbers from those years showed that they in fact did. What PharmaCo wasn't counting on was the *increase* in Cytoflux sales from 2000 to 2005 (Exhibit 12). Pricing didn't change and none of the other congestive heart failure drugs went off the market during that time period. Accounting errors aside, there had to be something driving those numbers.

She had pulled a second file regarding Cytoflux patient numbers in the archives, but it turned out to be equally confusing (Exhibit 13). It indicated that the audited numbers of patients from the data vendor did not match up with the numbers from the epidemiology and market research projections. At the time, it occurred to her that this could lead to two separate calculations for patient share. The list of puzzles goes on and on, and not just with Cytoflux.

Anna had been able to sort out many of these discrepancies in her six months as Forecasting Director, yet she still felt relatively new to the game. Now as she sat at her desk, the reddening sky outside bathed her office with a warm, sleepy hue. She removed her glasses and rubbed her eyes in circles, elbows balancing on the table…

The list of puzzles goes on and on.

Class	Product	Indication	Launch date	Exclusivity expiration date	Form
COX-2 Inhibitor	Orthonova	Acute osteoarthritis pain	Jan-06	Jan-20	Once-daily tablet
Beta-blocker	Cytoflux	Congestive heart failure	Jan-01	Jan-11	Once-daily tablet
SSRI	Verdantin	Chronic mild depression, obsessive-compulsive disorder, panic disorder, social anxiety disorder	Jan-95	Jan-07	Once-daily tablet
SSRI	Verdantin QW	Chronic mild depression, obsessive-compulsive disorder, panic disorder, social anxiety disorder	Jun-06	Mar-07	Once-weekly tablet
Antibiotic	Listromycin	Acute post-operative infection	Jan-94	Jun-05	Injectable

Exhibit 1   Product summaries

Question 1: Demand sales for Cytoflux (diamond line) reveal a fairly steady and smooth increase over time, while ex-factory sales (triangle line) are characterised by spikes, dips and cyclical variation. (Demand sales are calculated using audited retail and non-retail units for Cytoflux and applying ex-factory price to these audited data.) What are some possible causes for this? What are some ways that Anna might be able to correct for this in the analysis?

Question 2: To what extent are these cycles under the control of PharmaCo and how might it manage them?

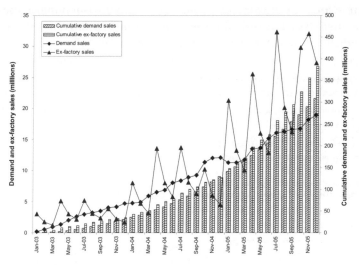

Exhibit 2.1   Ex-factory versus demand sales

Question 3: In estimating the 2006 sales for Cytoflux there are various historical time periods that can be used to project out the demand sales; namely, trending the data using a linear fit of the last 12 months, last 24 months and all 36 months of sales respectively. Based on the resulting R^2 value, which method seems the best predictor of 2006 sales? What does the R^2 value tell us? (The R^2 data for the various projections are: 12 months of data, $R^2 = 0.969$; 24 months of data, $R^2 = 0.977$; and 36 months of data, $R^2 = 0.983$.)

Question 4: Exhibit 2.2 projects both the ex-factory sales and demand sales data using the full 36 months of historical data using a linear fit. What should Anna use to estimate shipments for 2006?

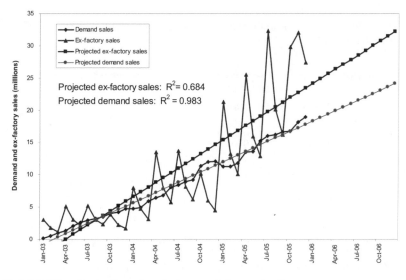

Projected ex-factory sales: $R^2 = 0.684$
Projected demand sales: $R^2 = 0.983$

Exhibit 2.2   Projection of ex-factory and demand sales

Question 5: *There seems to be a growing gap between cumulative ex-factory sales (right bars) and cumulative demand sales (left bars). What are possible causes of this? Is it something that should concern Anna?*

Patient therapy days for currently marketed products
Audited number of patient therapy days

	2005
Cartilin	300,000
Neoset	19,914
Arthrotone	77,254

Note: Obtained from days of therapy audits

Theoretical days of therapy per patient
Number of days of therapy a fully compliant patient receives

	2005
Cartilin	7
Neoset	4
Arthrotone	2

Note: Obtained from product labels

Patient data
Projected number of patients

	2005	2006	2007	2008	2009	2010
Orthonova		6,000	29,900	39,200	43,500	48,000
Cartilin	62,702	73,053	72,890	72,015	75,185	80,000
Neoset	6,638	12,757	29,756	48,537	58,279	64,000
Androne	40,660	34,190	27,354	19,448	16,536	16,000

Note: Obtained from long-term forecast model

Exhibit 3.1   Patient to TRx conversion

Question 6: *In a patient-based forecast, the result of a market share calculation is the number of patients on each product. Discuss reasons why we might be interested in calculating days of therapy or TRxes by product.*

Question 7: *Using the audited days of therapy for Cartilin in 2005, calculate the following:*

(A) average days of therapy per patient on Cartilin in 2005.

(B) overall compliance in 2005.

(C) Forecast days of therapy for Orthonova for 2006 to 2010 (make the assumption that the average days of therapy per patient and compliance remain constant over time).

Question 8: *Calculate the minimum volume of product that must be produced to satisfy the demand suggested by the calculation in Question 7C for 2006.*

Question 9: *Are there additional factors that Anna should take into account in converting patients to days of therapy?*

Question 10: *What are some problems with the calculation in Question 8? Would you expect a demand calculation based solely on epidemiology to accurately reflect ex-factory demand? Why or why not? Second, what factors other than patient-based demand might affect the volume of product that should be produced?*

	2000	2001	2002	2003	2004	2005
Verdantin patients (millions)	10.0	12.4	19.9	22.5	24.8	30.1
Verdantin TRx (millions)	80.4	96.2	152.1	154.3	144.3	150.7
Verdantin TRx per patient	8.0	7.8	7.6	6.9	5.8	5.0

Note: Patient data from long-term forecast; TRx data from audits

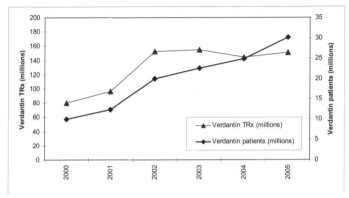

Exhibit 4   Patient and TRx trends

Question 11: *Despite a marked increase in the number of treated patients for Verdantin, the total market TRx (retail and non-retail) have been declining. What are some possible explanations?*

Question 12: *What additional information should Anna collect to help explain this?*

Question 13: *What measures might the product managers take to help capitalise on the increase in patients?*

	2000	2001	2002	2003	2004
Cytoflux TRx (millions)	0.6	0.9	1.4	1.8	2.2
Cytoflux demand sales (millions)	6.6	10.8	16.7	23.0	32.0
Cytoflux revenue per TRx	11.2	11.5	11.8	12.8	14.5

Note: TRx and demand sales data from audits

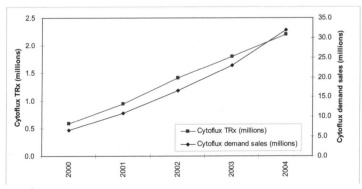

Exhibit 5   Demand sales and TRx trends

PHARMACO
– A FORECASTING
CASE STUDY

Question 14: *How do you explain the growing difference between TRx data and demand sales? Is this desirable? How might PharmaCo maintain (or reduce) this trend?*

Question 15: *What additional information should Anna collect to assist in explaining this?*

	2000	2001	2002	2003	2004	2005
Osteoarthritis market TRx (millions)	100	110	112	122	140	190
Osteoarthritis market days of therapy (millions)	2,900	3,012	2,950	2,991	2,520	2,850
Market DOT per TRx	29.0	27.4	26.3	24.5	18.0	15.0

Note: Data from audits

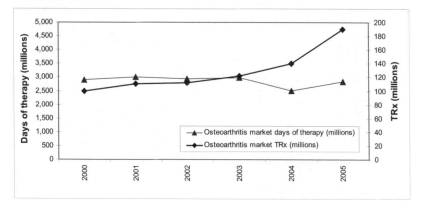

Exhibit 6   Market TRx to days of therapy

Question 16: *The market TRxes have grown at a healthy rate for the past two years, while the days of therapy have lagged. What are some possible explanations?*

Question 17: *What additional information should Anna collect to help track down the cause of this gap?*

Cannibalisation Table

Percent of patients on Verdatin who will switch to Verdantin QW

	2005	2006	2007	2008	2009	2010
Switching percentage	0	40	65	70	80	85

Note: Assumptions from long-term forecast model

Drug-treated patients

(millions)	2005	2006	2007	2008	2009	2010
Verdantin	30.0	35.0	10.0	4.0	2.0	1.5
Paxor	100.0	115.0	119.0	119.5	120.0	121.0
Prozan	105.0	110.0	95.0	75.0	43.0	22.0
Zolofan	85.0	86.0	84.0	87.0	88.0	86.5
TOTAL	**320.0**	**346.0**	**308.0**	**285.5**	**253.0**	**231.0**

Drug-treated patients by product (with line extension launch)

(millions)	2005	2006	2007	2008	2009	2010
Verdantin	30.0	21.0	3.5	1.2	0.4	0.2
Verdantin QW	0.0	14.0	6.5	2.8	1.6	1.3
Paxor	100.0	115.0	119.0	119.5	120.0	121.0
Prozan	105.0	110.0	95.0	75.0	43.0	22.0
Zolofan	85.0	86.0	84.0	87.0	88.0	86.5
TOTAL	**320.0**	**346.0**	**308.0**	**285.5**	**253.0**	**231.0**

Exhibit 7   Cannibalisation

Question 18: *Explain why cannibalisation can be a problem when a new formulation is launched for an existing product. Explain how it could potentially be advantageous.*

Question 19: *Why do you think the new formulation of Verdantin so readily cannibalises the patient share of the older formulation? Give two reasons.*

Question 20: *Based on what you see in these tables, is it worthwhile to pursue the new form? Why or why not?*

Generic erosion table
Percentage of patients on brand Listromycin relative to its volume before inhibitin launch

	2003	2004	2005	2006	2007	2008
Generic erosion rate	0%	0%	10%	59%	68%	70%
Retention rate	100%	100%	90%	41%	32%	30%

Note: Assumptions from long-term forecast model

Drug-treated patients

(millions)	2003	2004	2005	2006	2007	2008
Listromycin	15.0	17.5	16.4	14.0	14.0	12.0
Disinfex	50.0	57.5	59.5	59.8	60.0	60.5
Steromycin	52.5	55.0	47.5	37.5	21.5	11.0
Clensor	42.5	43.0	42.0	43.5	44.0	43.3
TOTAL	**160.0**	**173.0**	**165.4**	**154.8**	**139.5**	**126.8**

Drug-treated patients (with generic launch)

(millions)	2003	2004	2005	2006	2007	2008
Listromycin	15.0	17.5	14.8	5.7	4.5	3.6
inhibitin	0.0	0.0	1.6	8.3	9.5	8.4
Disinfex	50.0	57.5	59.5	59.8	60.0	60.5
Steromycin	52.5	55.0	47.5	37.5	21.5	11.0
Clensor	42.5	43.0	42.0	43.5	44.0	43.3
TOTAL	**160.0**	**173.0**	**165.4**	**154.8**	**139.5**	**126.8**

Exhibit 8   Generic erosion

Question 21: *Discuss how generic erosion and cannibalisation are similar.*

Question 22: *How can efforts to combat generic erosion lead to the need to forecast cannibalisation?*

	2000	2001	2002	2003	2004	2005
Prevalent population (thousands)	416.0	395.2	375.4	356.7	338.8	321.9
Diagnosed patients (thousands)	216.3	221.3	240.3	256.8	271.1	283.3
Diagnosis rate	52%	56%	64%	72%	80%	88%

Note: Data from epidemiology database

	2000	2001	2002	2003	2004	2005
Diagnosed patients (thousands)	216.3	221.3	240.3	256.8	271.1	283.3
Drug-treated patients (thousands)	132.2	135.0	132.2	129.3	123.5	110.0
Drug treatment rate	61%	61%	55%	50%	46%	39%

Note: Diagnosed patients from epidemiology database; drug treated patients calculated from audits

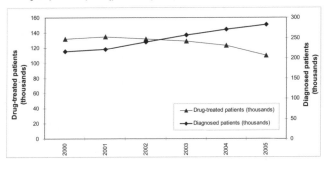

Exhibit 9   Epidemiology

Question 23: *From the graph, diagnosis rates are growing, however total drug-treated patients are decreasing. What are some possible explanations for this observation?*

Question 24: *What is the best approach to evaluate the commercial opportunities for a new drug – patient or prescription models? List three to four benefits for each approach.*

Question 25: *If you were Anna, who would you pick to be on your forecast team, Kerre or Ruth? Support your decision.*

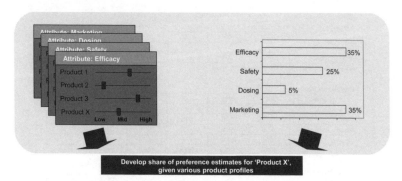

Exhibit 10   Estimating market share

Question 26: *In the attribute scoring methodology, patient share is assumed to be a function of product attributes and how the market values these attributes. Brainstorm some product attributes that could potentially be used to score a product. As you list, group the attributes by whether they are related to clinical features of the product, or commercial features.*

Question 27: *Why is it useful to view a product as a collection of individual attributes when you are trying to estimate its future market share?*

Question 28: *Do you think it's possible to score a product across too many attributes? At what point might increasing the number of attributes detract from the insight of your forecast?*

	Jan	Feb	Mar	Apr	May	Jun	Jul	Aug	Sep	Oct	Nov	Dec
Projected share	0.0%	1.0%	2.0%	3.0%	4.0%	5.0%	6.0%	7.0%	8.0%	9.0%	10.0%	11.0%
Actual share	0.0%	0.5%	0.5%	0.5%	1.0%	1.5%	8.0%	10.0%	11.0%	11.5%	12.0%	12.3%

Note: Data from long-term forecast and TRx audits

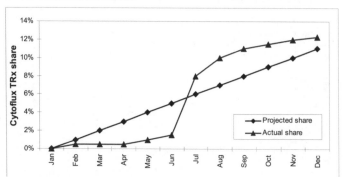

Exhibit 11   Market share projection trends

Question 29: *Think of a few reasons that might explain why the curves in Exhibit 11 are shaped so differently.*

Question 30: *What questions might Anna try to answer to generate an accurate projection for Orthonova? In other words, what are some of the sources of information she could use to judge how Orthonova's share is likely to change in the year of its launch?*

	2001	2002	2003	2004	2005
Cytoflux patients (thousands)	50.0	50.1	50.1	50.2	50.3
Cytoflux ex-factory sales (millions)	27.4	30.6	33.0	35.4	37.8
Revenue per patient	547.50	610.92	657.91	704.91	751.90

Note: Patient data calculated from retail audits; ex-factory sales from Finance

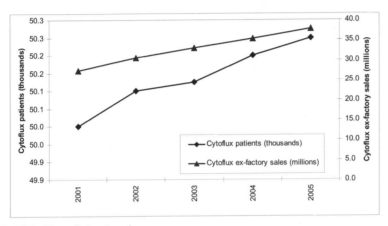

Exhibit 12 Sales trends

Question 31: *What are some possible explanations for why the sales trend for Cytoflux does not match the patient trend?*

Question 32: *What would be a potential hazard of modelling sales solely on epidemiological factors?*

Audited patient counts	2005
Cytoflux	25
Decongestex	25
Angiodine	50
TOTAL	100

Note: Data calculated from audits

Epidemiology patient counts	2005
Total treated patients	75

Note: Data from epidemiology and market research studies

	Share calculated from audited data (%)	Share calculated from epidemiology data (%)
Cytoflux	25	33
Decongestex	25	33
Angiodine	50	67
TOTAL	100	133

Exhibit 13 Reconciling patient totals

PHARMACO
– A FORECASTING
CASE STUDY

Question 33: *How can Anna reconcile that the epidemiology and market research reflect different patient totals than the sum of audited patient counts by product? What are some possible explanations for this?*

Question 34: *How should she compute and project market share?*

SUGGESTED ANSWERS

The following are suggested answers for the questions posed in the case study. These are by no means the only possible answers, and readers are encouraged to offer alternative solutions.

Question 1: Demand sales for Cytoflux (diamond line) reveal a fairly steady and smooth increase over time, while ex-factory sales (triangle line) are characterised by spikes, dips and cyclical variation. (Demand sales are calculated using audited retail and non-retail units for Cytoflux and applying ex-factory price to these audited data.) What are some possible causes for this? What are some ways that Anna might be able to correct for this in the analysis?

- There may be a change in the distribution channels, with more product moving through unaudited channels. If this were the case, ex-factory sales would also capture the demand in the unaudited channels, whereas audited data would not capture these additional, non-audited units.

- Variations also could be due to distributor purchase patterns. Note the cyclical nature of the spikes; this may be in anticipation of price increases.

- Another possible explanation is internal 'gaming' on the part of PharmaCo managers seeking to achieve goals and/or manage budgets. Note that the cycles are every three months corresponding to quarters.

- Anna might be able to better gauge if these dynamics are operating in the market by:
  a. reviewing any available data in the unaudited channels to determine if these channels account for additional (and increasing) demand;
  b. examining distributor inventories; and
  c. overlaying price increases on top of the above data to see if price speculation is operating.

Question 2: To what extent are these cycles under the control of PharmaCo and how might it manage them?

- To the extent that there is internal gaming, PharmaCo could provide disincentives to discourage this behaviour, or incentives that are tied to ensuring smoother sales patterns.

- If the pattern is the result of distributor buying activity, PharmaCo has less control, but may be able to analyse the timing of the spikes and plan accordingly. As noted above, distributor speculation purchases often occurs as the result of anticipated price increases. Inventory management agreements with the distributors may smooth out the ex-factory sales pattern.

Question 3: In estimating the 2006 sales for Cytoflux there are various historical time periods that can be used to project out the demand sales; namely, trending the data using a linear fit of the last 12 months, last 24 months and all 36 months of sales respectively. Based on the resulting

PHARMACO
– A FORECASTING
CASE STUDY

R^2 value, which method seems the best predictor of 2006 sales? What does the R^2 value tell us? (The R^2 data for the various projections are: 12 months of data, $R^2 = 0.969$; 24 months of data, $R^2 = 0.977$; and 36 months of data, $R^2 = 0.983$.)

- The R^2 of a regression model, also known as the correlation coefficient, is a measure of the variance in the data that is explained by the regression used in trending. If the regression is a strong positively correlated fit, R^2 approaches 1.0, and if the regression is a strong negatively correlated fit, R^2 approaches -1.0. If $R^2 = 0$ there is no definite relationship between the data and the fitted line.

- In general, one should use all relevant data and more data are preferable. In the above example, using longer time period results seems to produce a better projection of 2006 demand sales as the R^2 value is highest for the fit using 36 months of data. However, Anna must decide what data are relevant. Older data tend to be less relevant than recent data and one must adjust for important events that occurred in the past. For example, if Cytoflux obtained new indications in 2004, historical sales in 2003 will be irrelevant for projecting sales in 2006.

Question 4: Exhibit 2.2 projects both the ex-factory sales and demand sales data using the full 36 months of historical data using a linear fit. What should Anna use to estimate shipments for 2006?

- Using the criterion of highest R^2 value indicating the best fit, Anna would choose the demand sales trend line. These data have less variation than the ex-factory sales data. Projection of the demand sales data provides a baseline for the demand for audited channels in the future.

- However, if Anna needs to estimate shipments from PharmaCo in the future she needs to modify this projection to account for the discrepancy between demand and ex-factory sales. If the historical trend continues, she may use the ex-factory sales data and projection as a gauge of future shipments (the projection line illustrated on the graph above). If she believes the difference between demand and ex-factory sales will diminish in the future she should use a projection value lower than the projected ex-factory sales, but higher than the projected demand sales – namely, a range between the two.

Question 5: There seems to be a growing gap between cumulative ex-factory sales (right bars) and cumulative demand sales (left bars). What are possible causes of this? Is it something that should concern Anna?

- One possible explanation for the growing gap is that distributors are increasing inventory (something that can be measured and accounted for) or hiding inventory in speculation warehouses in anticipation of future price increases (more difficult to assess). Any increases to distributor inventory put future PharmaCo sales at risk, as sales will drop when the distributor releases the inventory. The magnitude of these at-risk sales is given by the difference between cumulative demand and cumulative ex-factory sales. This should definitely concern Anna.

- Another possibility is gaps in the data. Audits are imperfect. They do not capture all channels nor do they capture a full census of the distribution channels. The data need to be bulked-up to account for this. If the bulk-up factor is insufficient, the result will be a growing gap between the audits and internal sales measures.

Question 6: In a patient-based forecast, the result of a market share calculation is the number of patients on each product. Discuss reasons why we might be interested in calculating days of therapy or TRxes by product.

- Days of therapy and TRx are measured data and therefore easier to validate using audit sources. The calculated values in the historical year (from the forecast model) should be close to the historical values (from the audits).

- Days of therapy and TRx data are more useful for determining production requirements since they are more readily converted to units.

- In most therapy areas, either days of therapy and TRx data are more readily converted to revenue than patients.

Question 7: Using the audited days of therapy for Cartilin in 2005, calculate the following:

(A) average days of therapy per patient on Cartilin in 2005.

- $300,000 \div 62,702 = 4.78$

(B) overall compliance in 2005.

- Compliance = average days of therapy divided by theoretical days of therapy.
  or $4.78 \div 7 = 68\%$

- Alternatively, compliance = audited number of therapy days divided by theoretical number of therapy days, where the theoretical number of therapy days equals the total patients multiplied by theoretical days of therapy per patient.

- $300,000 \div (62,702*7) = 68\%$

(C) Forecast days of therapy for Orthonova for 2006–2010 (make the assumption that the average days of therapy per patient and compliance remain constant over time).

- Days of therapy = patients multiplied by theoretical days of therapy multiplied by compliance.

Days of therapy for Orthonova

	2005	2006	2007	2008	2009	2010
Orthonova patients		6,000	29,900	39,200	43,500	48,000
Theoretical days of therapy		7	7	7	7	7
Compliance		68%	68%	68%	68%	68%
Days of therapy		28,707	143,058	187,554	208,127	229,658

Exhibit 3.2 Calculation of days of therapy for Orthonova

PHARMACO
– A FORECASTING
CASE STUDY

Question 8: Calculate the minimum volume of product that must be produced to satisfy the demand suggested by the calculation in Question 7C for 2006.

- Assuming once daily dosing for 2006:
  a. 1 day of therapy = 1 pill
  b. 1 pill multiplied by 28,707 days of therapy = 28,707 pills in 2006
- Another approach is to say that the minimum production values must satisfy the number of TRxes written, regardless of compliance. This assumes that patients do not save unused medication and receive a full seven day script for every episode. In this case the minimum production units would be:

  7 days of therapy multiplied by 6,000 patients = 42,000 pills.

Question 9: Are there additional factors that Anna should take into account in converting patients to days of therapy?

- The above calculations do not account for persistence.
- Other potential issues that Anna might consider are dosing splits and any titration issues.

Question 10: What are some problems with the calculation in Question 8? Would you expect a demand calculation based solely on epidemiology to accurately reflect ex-factory demand? Why or why not? Second, what factors other than patient-based demand might affect the volume of product that should be produced?

- The calculations in Question 8 reflect the minimum acceptable amount.
- Other factors that must be considered are:
  a. distributor demand, which is not completely governed by epidemiological demand. Distributors may include wholesalers, hospitals, care facilities, and pharmacies.
  b. manufacturing demand, such as safety stock and PharmaCo inventories.

Question 11: Despite a marked increase in the number of treated patients for Verdantin, the total market TRx (retail and non-retail) have been declining. What are some possible explanations?

- This can be due to decreased compliance or persistence, where patients are not receiving refill prescriptions in a timely manner.
- The ratio may be changing because of increased sampling, where potential TRxes are being replaced by samples.
- Another explanation is an increase in the average size of the TRx being written. This would be true if more of the TRx are bring dispensed through channels such as mail-order, where the average TRx size is larger.

Question 12: What additional information should Anna collect to help explain this?

- Data for compliance and persistence trends, sampling levels and average TRx size would be helpful in analysing the situation and projecting future changes.

Question 13: What measures might the product managers take to help capitalise on the increase in patients?

- Patient education (perhaps direct-to-consumer marketing) and increased marketing to physicians to capture more of the expanding market. In other words, make efforts to increase compliance and persistence (and thus the value of each patient) if there is a compliance or persistence issue.
- If prescriptions are being lost due to sampling PharmaCo can decrease the number of samples.
- If a change in the length of the TRx is the reason for the decrease, there is no action needed by product management (assuming the value of the TRx rises as the size increases).

Question 14: How do you explain the growing difference between TRx data and demand sales? Is this desirable? How might PharmaCo maintain (or reduce) this trend?

- Overall this is a desirable trend for Cytoflux, as the revenue per TRx is increasing every year. (Note that the choice of the two y-axes is responsible for the cross-over of the trend lines in 2005.)
- Increasing difference between dollar sales and TRx likely is due to one (or more) of the following:
  a. higher prescription length.
  b. up titration of the daily dose for Cytoflux, leading to increased consumption of product.
  c. Note that the case study mentioned that pricing for Cytoflux did not change during this period; otherwise a price increase would have been a reasonable explanation.

Question 15: What additional information should Anna collect to assist in explaining this?

- Anna should analyse average daily dosing and prescription length.

Question 16: The market TRxes have grown at a healthy rate for the past two years, while the days of therapy have lagged. What are some possible explanations?

- This decreases in day of therapy may be due to a new entrant with a longer length of therapy – for example, once-weekly dosing which replaces once daily-dosing. This could mean that it would require fewer prescriptions to treat the same number, or a greater number of patients.

Question 17: What additional information should Anna collect to help track down the cause of this gap?

- Product-level data would help identify this. In particular, has there been a new product launched recently with a dramatically different length of therapy than existing products? What do prescribing patterns look like? Is the length of script changing?

Question 18: Explain why cannibalisation can be a problem when a new formulation is launched for an existing product. Explain how it could potentially be advantageous.

- Cannibalisation of an existing formulation by a new formulation may hinder the share of the existing product. The new formulation essentially steals share from the old one, which may not increase overall company revenues if there is no economic advantage to the new formulation.
- Cannibalisation can be beneficial if the aim was to transfer patients off a product that is approaching patent expiry to a new product or formulation with a longer patent life. In this case the company obtains economic benefit by avoiding the price erosion typically seen when a product loses marketing exclusivity and generics enter the market.
- Cannibalisation also can provide benefits to both patients and a company's reputation when the new formulation brings advantages to the patient – such as increased efficacy, tolerability, or compliance.

Question 19: Why do you think the new formulation of Verdantin so readily cannibalises the patient share of the older formulation? Give two reasons.

- This probably occurs because Verdantin is approaching patent expiry and the marketing efforts for the current formulation may have been abandoned.
- Another possibility is that if the new formulation of Verdantin represents an improvement in dosing and convenience, it is more likely to take share from its inferior predecessor.

Question 20: Based on what you see in these tables, is it worthwhile to pursue the new form? Why or why not?

- The numbers in the third table do not show an increase over the sales PharmaCo would have achieved had they kept only the old formulation; nor do they show any gain in share from other competitors in the market. Because launch is more expensive than maintaining a current product, these numbers suggest that, unless this represents a patent extension strategy, a significant economic advantage, or benefits to the patients it would be wise to forgo the launch of the new formulation of Verdantin QW.

Question 21: Discuss how generic erosion and cannibalisation are similar.

- Generic erosion occurs when the generic version of a branded product enters the market environment and steals share from the brand. Cannibalisation occurs when a new entry steals share from an incumbent due to similarity of their markets. They can both be modelled similarly because in each case, the amounts of share stolen and the products the share will be transferred between follow similar trends.

Question 22: How can efforts to combat generic erosion lead to the need to forecast cannibalisation?

- Most lifecycle management strategies involve new formulations or dosage that extends the patent life. One such example – as illustrated in Exhibit 8 – might be the shift from daily to weekly dosing.

Question 23: From the graph, diagnosis rates are growing, however total drug-treated patients are decreasing. What are some possible explanations for this observation?

- New non-prescription treatment alternatives – for example, surgery, medical devices, over-the-counter drugs, or alternative medicine – may have entered the market and be competing with prescription drug treatments.
- Current prescription therapies are proving to be unsuccessful hence physicians may not be willing to prescribe prescription therapies.
- A change in treatment guidelines may call for non-prescription interventions – such as diet and exercise – prior to placing the patient on prescription drug therapies.

Question 24: What is the best approach to evaluate the commercial opportunities for a new drug – patient or prescription models? List three or four benefits for each approach.

- Patient models will:
  a. allow you to model the entire market for a disease.
  b. enable modelling of growth rates through increased diagnosis or drug treatment rates.
  c. allow for white space or undeveloped disease areas (for example, emerging or new therapies).
  d. decompose the opportunities better on all variables (for example, persistence).
  e. model all indications separately to assess their potential.
- On the other hand, prescription models:
  a. reflect the data reported by the audits and are thus readily calibrated.
  b. use the best measurable information for the currently treated market.
  c. have compliance and persistence rates inherent in the data.
  d. require fewer assumptions.
  e. often require factoring of Rx data if the model is indication-specific.

Question 25: If you were Anna, who would you pick to be on your forecast team, Kerre or Ruth? Support your decision.

- There is no absolute answer for this question, although patient-based models arguably are generally better suited for development products because of their ability to link to epidemiology sources. In general, patient-based forecast models more accurately reflect the dynamics in the market by acknowledging all of the competition and forecasting at the indication level. On the other hand, they take more time and resources and require a larger number of judgemental assumptions. Any patient-based model will have a prescription component where prescriptions are converted to patients and used to calibrate the market share to historical audits.
- Prescription-based models begin with audited data and are therefore easier to calibrate in the market. When a product is used across multiple indications and the forecaster is not concerned with use by indication, prescription-based models provide a simpler forecast construct. Also, there is no need to assume compliance and persistence rates, as these are inherent in the actual data.
- If possible Anna should strive to hire both individuals.

Question 26: In the attribute scoring methodology, patient share is assumed to be a function of product attributes and how the market values these attributes. Brainstorm some product attributes that could potentially be used to score a product. As you list, group the attributes by whether they are related to clinical features of the product, or commercial features.

- Example clinical attributes:
    a. efficacy
    b. safety
    c. tolerability
    d. side-effects
    e. symptom relief
    f. onset of action
    g. dosing and convenience.
- Example commercial attributes:
    a. price
    b. marketing effort
    c. therapy area franchise
    d. sales force effort
    e. breadth of claim
    f. dosing and convenience.

Question 27: Why is it useful to view a product as a collection of individual attributes when you are trying to estimate its future market share?

- Breaking a product down into individual attributes makes it easier to compare products in the market environment on the basis of measurable parameters. It also allows you to identify reasons why one product may be prescribed more often than another, which in turn allows you to make more informed marketing decisions. This approach hinges on the concept that a product is the sum of its attributes, and that the perception of a product is the sum of the perception of its attributes. This approach also best leverages the results of market research studies, such as discrete choice or conjoint analyses.

Question 28: Do you think it's possible to score a product across too many attributes? At what point might increasing the number of attributes detract from the insight of your forecast?

- If you decompose a product into too many attributes, changing the value of any one attribute score will have less effect overall. Data collection will also be more difficult because clinical experts will need to score more attributes during a scoring session. A good rule of thumb is to limit the number of attributes to six or seven. It is unlikely that physicians consider more than this when making a prescribing decision.

Question 29: Think of a few reasons that might explain why the curves in Exhibit 11 are shaped so differently.

- The projected share is linear, which is the simplest way to view share projection. The real data shows that there was initially slow uptake, followed by a rapid phase, and then a levelling off.
- Many products require months or years to establish awareness in the market, leading to a slower uptake in the initial months after launch. Promotional efforts, such as segmentation and targeting, can accelerate an adoption pattern.
- The slower adoption pattern also could be due to insufficient marketing efforts at first, followed by a large increase around the June time period.
- The forecast curve may have been modelled using a faulty analogue. Different market environment circumstances can result in different uptakes.
- Perhaps a critical Phase IV study was released in May/June resulting in accelerated uptake due to the results of the study.

Question 30: What questions might Anna try to answer to generate an accurate projection for Orthonova? In other words, what are some of the sources of information she could use to judge how Orthonova's share is likely to change in the year of its launch?

- What is the expected total share in 2007?
- What is the expected total share after 12, 24 and 36 months?
- What is the competitive market share and what is a good analogue with which to model share?
- What resources will PharmaCo invest in promotion?
- What are the resource and launch assumptions about the competitors?

Question 31: What are some possible explanations for why the sales trend for Cytoflux does not match the patient trend?

- One possibility is that the percentage of sales by indication is changing, moving from acute indications to more chronic indications. It is possible that doctors prescribed Cytoflux for something more acute than congestive heart failure, which is a chronic condition, and then shifted prescribing patterns toward more chronic indications. A more common example might occur with anti-infectives, for acute sinusitis to chronic sinusitis.
- Another possibility is increased compliance/persistence.
- Increases in either price or average dosage also would explain this type of trend.

Question 32: What would be a potential hazard of modelling sales solely on epidemiological factors?

- There is always the danger of neglecting important market and economic factors that are independent of epidemiological factors – such as the promotional activities behind the product.
- Epidemiology data must be calibrated to historical prescription and/or unit data from the audits to validate the model construct.

Question 33: How can Anna reconcile that the epidemiology and market research reflect different patient totals than the sum of audited patient counts by product? What are some possible explanations for this?

- Part of the difference may be due to uncertainty around the different data sources.
- Another strong possibility (given the large discrepancy) is polypharmacy or concominant therapy. In the congestive heart failure market, it is common for a patient to be treated with multiple drugs for the same condition. With audited data, this can lead to the same patient being counted multiple times. The results are a greater number of patients from the audited totals than from the epidemiology data.

Question 34: How should she compute and project market share?

- The numerator of the share calculation should always be the number of patients on each product. For the denominator, she could either use the total audited patient counts, or use the drug treated patient pool. In the first instance, the result is share of patient equivalents or product patients. In the second instance, patients are double-counted and the result is share of treated patients. Thus, both calculations in Exhibit 13 are valid, but measure different share values.

Appendix: Forecast Techniques

JUDGEMENT TOOLS

Historical analogy

Predictions based on elements of past events that are analogous to the present situation.

Naive extrapolation

Application of a simple assumption about a future outcome, or a simple subjective extension of the results of current events.

Delphi

Forecasting through group consensus involving anonymity, iteration and controlled feedback. Delphi is most appropriate where the question under consideration is so complex and involves such obscure relationships that no single person could be expected to be expert in the many disciplines required. The value of the results depends largely on the excellence and cooperation of the participants

Scenario

A description of an internally consistent, plausible future. A scenario does not purport to be a prediction; rather, it provides a framework in which the consequences and effectiveness of potential management decisions can be evaluated.

Expert workshop

A form of Delphi where expert opinion is elicited and aggregated in an interactive environment. Besides the Delphi consensus decision, the interactions between experts are part of the forecasting process.

Cross-impact

Assesses the interdependence of future events where the chance of occurrence of one event depends strongly on the probability of another interrelated event occurring.

COUNTING TOOLS

Secondary data

Purchase intentions are estimated based on historical data that have been collected for similar products and markets.

Primary market research

Attitudinal and purchase intentions are gathered from representative decision-makers. The data are extrapolated to estimate a product's future prospects.

Conjoint

Survey method that measures the importance of a product's attributes in the consumer's mind and quantifies trade-offs between these attributes.

TIME SERIES TOOLS

Moving average

Recent values of the forecast variables averaged to predict future outcomes.

Smoothing

An estimate for the coming period based on a mathematically weighted combination of the actual and estimated outcomes of the previous period. Unlike moving averages this technique uses all the preceding observations to determine a smoothed value for a particular time period. Reliance is placed on more recent data. A smoothing factor can be introduced to dampen changes suggested by the most recent datapoints. Holt-Winters (with seasonality) is the most frequently used exponential smoothing model in the pharmaceutical industry.

Adaptive filtering

A derivation of exponential smoothing in which the model has been altered systematically to reflect data pattern changes.

Decomposition

A prediction of expected outcomes from trend, seasonal, cyclical and random components that are determined independently from the data series to be forecast.

Trend extrapolation

A prediction of future outcomes derived from the extension of a mathematical function, using time as the independent variable, that has been fitted to a data series. Also referred to as autoregression.

ARIMA

Autogregressive Integrated Moving Average models, the most familiar of which is the Box-Jenkins model. These are complex, computer-based iterative procedures that produce time series forecasting models based on autoregressive, stationary, moving average models.

CAUSAL TOOLS

Correlation

Predictions of future values based on the historic patterns of covariation and dependence between input variables. Correlation does not necessarily imply causality.

Regression

Estimates produced by a predictive equation derived by minimising the residual variance of one or more predictor (independent) variables. For example, if company sales were to be forecast, they might be dependent on time, the economy, the number of sales calls, promotional activity and so forth.

Leading indicators

Assumes one trend can be derived from another, often by application of a simple lead–lag relationship. For example, forecasting sales dollars for one month based on the advertising expenditures in a prior month.

Input–output

A matrix model that indicates how demand changes in one area can directly and cumulatively affect other areas.

Econometric

Future values forecast from an integrated system of simultaneous equations that represent the relationships among the input variables.

Vector autoregression

One of the newest and most complex computer-based forecasting models, this is a dynamic econometric model in which several equations are forecast simultaneously.

References and Further Reading

Abt, R., Borja, M., Menke, M. M. and Pezier, J. P. (1979) 'The Dangerous Quest for Certainty in Market Forecasting', *Long Range Planning*, 12, 287–96.

Amara, R. (1989) 'A Note on What We Have Learned About the Methods of Futures Planning', *Technological Forecasting and Social Change*, 36, 43–7.

Armstrong, J. S. (1985) *Long-range Forecasting from Crystal Ball to Computer,* 2nd edn, New York: John Wiley & Sons.

Armstrong, J. S. (ed.) (2001) *Principles of Forecasting: A Handbook for Researchers and Practitioners*, Norwell: Kluwer Academic Publishers.

Chambers, J. C., Mullick, S. K. and Smith, D. D. (1971) 'How to Choose the Right Forecasting Technique', *Harvard Business Review*, July–August, 45–74.

Chase, C. W. (1992) 'The Effects of Corporate Politics on Business Forecasting', *The Journal of Business Forecasting*, Winter 1991–1992, 6–8.

Coates, J. F. (1989) 'Forecasting and Planning Today Plus or Minus Twenty Years', *Technological Forecasting and Social Change*, 36, 15–20.

Coates, J. F. and Jarratt, J. (1989) *What Futurists Believe*, Mt. Airy: Lomond Publications, Inc.

Cook, A. G. (1990) 'Taking the Fuzzy Out of Forecasting as a Strategic Tool', *Pharmaceutical Executive*, December, 50–6.

Cook, A. G. (1991) 'Building the Future with the Forecaster's Toolbox', *Pharmaceutical Executive*, July, 48–54.

Cook, A. G. (1995) 'Navigating the Intersection of Forecasting, Market Research and Pricing', *Pharmaceutical Executive*, August, 54–8.

Ellis, D. and Nathan, J. (1990) *A Managerial Guide to Business Forecasting*, New York: Graceway Publishing Company, Inc.

Evans, M. K. (2003) *Practical Business Forecasting*, Oxford: Blackwell Publishers Ltd.

Georgoff, D. M. and Murdick, R. G. (1986) 'Manager's Guide to Forecasting', *Harvard Business Review*, January–February, 110–20.

Goodrich, R. L. (1989) *Applied Statistical Forecasting*, Belmont: Business Forecast Systems, Inc.

Gordon, T. J. (1989) 'Futures Research: Did It Meet Its Promise? Can it Meet Its Promise', *Technological Forecasting and Social Change*, 36, 21–6.

Humphreys, A. (2004) 'Future Blockbusters', *MedAdNews*, January, 1–12.

Jain, C. L. (ed.) (1987), *A Managerial Guide to Judgmental Forecasting*, New York: Graceway Publishing Company, Inc.

Jain, C. L. (ed.) (1988), *Understanding Business Forecasting*: 2nd edn, New York: Graceway Publishing Company, Inc.

Lapide, L. (2002) 'Where Should the Forecasting Function Reside?', *The Journal of Business Forecasting Methods & Systems*, Winter 2002–2003, 15–18.

Lidstone, J. and MacLennan, J. (1999) *Marketing Planning for the Pharmaceutical Industry*, 2nd edn, Aldershot: Gower Publishing Ltd.

MacLennan, J. (2004) *Brand Planning for the Pharmaceutical Industry*, Aldershot: Gower Publishing Ltd.

Mahaffie, J. B. (1995) 'Why Forecasts Fail', *American Demographics*, March, 34–40.

Makridakis, S., Wheelwright, S. C. and Hyndman, R. J. (1998) *Forecasting Methods and Applications*, 3rd edn, New York: John Wiley & Sons, Inc.

Maskus, K. E. (2001) *Parallel Imports in Pharmaceuticals: Implications for Competition and Prices in Developing Countries*. Available at http://www.wipo.int/about-ip/en/studies/pdf/ssa-maskus__pi.pdf#search='maskus%20parallel%20imports'.

Migliaro, A. and Jain, C. L. (eds) (1987) *An Executive's Guide to Econometric Forecasting*, New York: Graceway Publishing Company, Inc.

Newbold, P. and Bos, T. (1990) *Introductory Business Forecasting*, Cincinnati, OH: South-Western Publishing Company.

O'Boyle, J. (1999) *Wrong!: The Biggest Mistakes and Miscalculations Ever Made by People Who Should Have Known Better*, New York: Penguin Putnam, Inc.

Paich, M., Peck, C. and Valant, J. (2005) *Pharmaceutical Product Strategy: Using Dynamic Modeling for Effective Brand Planning*, Boca Raton, FL: CRC Press.

Riccardo, J. P. and Ryan, B. (1985) 'Minimizing the Risks', *Pharmaceutical Executive*, November, 74–6.

Rogers, E. M. (1962) *Diffusion of Innovations*, New York: The Free Press.

Rogers, M. J., Gupta, A. and Maranas, C. D. (2002) 'Real Options-based Analysis of Optimal Pharmaceutical Research and Development Portfolios', *Industrial Engineering and Chemical Research*, 41, 6607–20.

Shanklin, W. L. (1987) 'Six Timeless Marketing Blunders', *The Journal of Business and Industrial Marketing*, 2, 17–25.

Schnaars, S. P. (1989) *Megamistakes: Forecasting and the Myth of Rapid Technological Change*, New York: Macmillan, Inc.

Schrage, M. (1991) 'Spreadsheets Paper Over Real Problems', *Los Angeles Times*, 11 April, part D, p. 1.

The Health Strategies Consultancy LLC (2005) *Follow the Pill: Understanding the U.S. Pharmaceutical Supply Chain*, Menlo Park, CA: The Kaiser Family Foundation.

Wack, P. (1985) 'Scenarios: Unchartered Waters Ahead', *Harvard Business Review*, September–October, 73–89.

Wack, P. (1985) 'Scenarios: Shooting the Rapids', *Harvard Business Review*, November–December, 139–50.

Wallace, T. F. and Stahl, R. A. (2002) *Sales Forecasting: A New Approach*, Cincinnati, OH: T. F. Wallace & Company.

Zoltners, A. A., Sinha, P., and Lorimer, S. E. (2004) *Sales Force Design for Strategic Advantage*, Houndmills: Palgrave Macmillan.

Zoltners, A. A., Sinha, P. and Zoltners, G. A. (2001) *The Complete Guide to Accelerating Sales Force Performance*, New York: American Management Association.

REFERENCES AND
FURTHER READING

Index